# A MESSAGE FROM
# THE FALKLANDS

David in *Glamorgan*, Kiel June 1981

# A MESSAGE FROM THE FALKLANDS

The Life and Gallant Death
of David Tinker, Lieut.R.N.

*From his letters and poems*

Compiled by Hugh Tinker

Junction Books
London

First published in Great Britain by
Junction Books,
15 St John's Hill,
London SW11 1TN

ISBN 0 86245 102 7

Printed and bound in Great Britain by
Titus Wilson & Son Ltd., Kendal

Certainly the trivia of life and the important
things are all brought to mind by this. And
how much the trivia are at the forefront of
normal life and the important things put
away, or not done, or left to do later and then
forgotten. Here, certainly, the material things
are unimportant and human things, values,
and ways of life are thought about by
everybody.

*From* HMS GLAMORGAN, *22 May 1982*

Some readers may wish to turn first to the later letters
from the South Atlantic (pp. 168-201) which are the
essence of the message of this book.

FOR CHRISTINE

# The End and the Beginning

At about 6.30 p.m. on Sunday 13 June 1982 the telephone rang. Christine's voice said: "Hugh: I have some very bad news: David was killed yesterday". I could not say anything in reply. I staggered off and gasped the news out to Elisabeth, my wife. Numbed, dry-eyed, disbelieving, we sat staring at each other. Before dawn next morning the tears began to flow. Jonathan, our eldest son, and Helena his wife came as soon as they were able. After our first lamentations we began to talk of Dave. I showed them his letters from the Falklands, and especially the last letter (as then received) written on May 22nd. Helena said "That tells it all", and also "Other people ought to know what is in that letter".

Next morning (Tuesday) the first letters of condolence arrived. One from an Anglican priest read: "We know how unhappy you have been about this venture from the start and feel that with the authority that comes from your suffering you will be able to make a more important contribution to the restoration of a sane and humane attitude to the future in the South Atlantic." Helena read this and murmured, "That letter, that letter".

At that time I still felt quite unnerved, but I realised I ought to respond to Helena's urgings. I went away and thought. I am an author. The one thing I can do properly is to create books. I must make a book of my son's life showing how he, a very ordinary though a very lovely boy, arrived at the ideas and beliefs in his last letters. Then, through his letters, he could reach out and make known how he had come to grasp the meaning of the war in the South Atlantic. A life of David, through his letters . . . .

Christine had been taken to her home in Lydiate by her kind commanding officer and his wife. Her mother was to come out of hospital after a very severe operation on that Monday, 14 June, so she asked us to wait till next day to go and see her. We arrived at Lydiate on Tuesday afternoon. Her parents mourned for David as if for their own son. We were all so sad. I explained to Christine how I hoped to honour the

memory of David – and all the other men who died in the
Falklands battles. She accepted the idea gladly and offered to
show me some of her own letters from Dave.

*        *        *

The words above were set down within three or four days of
David's death. We then began to search for his letters. Most
were together in a bundle, but a few were scattered in different
places. A last precious few arrived from the Falklands, later.
We have had to wait some time for David's effects to be
released by the Navy, and (as this is written) have not seen his
poems written in the South Atlantic. A handful of his letters
remain undiscovered. Maybe they will turn up, too late for
inclusion.

David cannot be described as a regular correspondent, so
far as his parents were concerned. Sometimes, when he was
away he would not write for weeks and if one mildly reproached
him he would reply "There was nothing to write about".
When stimulated by some unusual experience, he could write
vividly, and often with a wry sense of humour. The letters to
us, which follow, reflect many different moods. Probably, most
frequently it is one of comedy. Dave's attitude to the armed
forces remained respectful yet irreverent. Concerned to cherish
and uphold tradition *when it is a living force* he refuses to accept
anything which is preserved merely because it has always been
so. He judges people not by their rank or office but by how
they employ their authority. And so we find him observing his
superiors with a mischievous eye. Those who are genuine
receive his respect, even if he does not always accept their
standards. There are others – Captains and Chief Petty
Officers alike – who are drawn as figures of fun. For most of
the sailors (not all) he has a liking and an understanding.
Dave sees them surviving difficulties and tribulations by
making a joke of it all. It is an attitude to which he also
subscribes.

A vein of poetry and gentle fantasy pervades his life, though
it is not often revealed in his letters to us. Though our
relationship is frank and friendly he does not often disclose his
inward thoughts. Sometimes these are revealed in whimsical
asides, as in his letter of 27 July 1980 where we glimpse his

feeling for the hidden world of nature: closer to him, perhaps, than the everyday world of men.

Inevitably, many letters are taken up with trivial comings and goings (what David when a tiny boy called 'rangements). Most of this is not included, though here and there unimportant exchanges are left in. These, after all, are not meant to be literary exercises: just the spontaneous – and often hastily written – letters of an ordinary young man to his parents.

Christine has numerous letters, and she has given access to many of them, with certain omissions. Much of what David writes to her is what a lover writes to the one he loves most. Although this is such an important part of his life it does not seem appropriate to include these thoughts alongside the letters written to his parents at a very different level of communication. Besides these most intimate exchanges there are other passages which have been omitted. For David, his wife is his refuge and strength. He writes to her when pressures seem unbearable, without holding anything back. In the confined circumstances of life on board ship these pressures build up, and relations with others may become strained. Dave sometimes writes about an individual in tones of exasperation when at other times he will write of him with tolerance and kindly feeling. It is difficult to get it right, but an attempt has been made to illustrate the element of doubt and frustration in David's life without over-emphasising the melancholy side of his nature. It is my belief that down amid the grey expanses of the South Atlantic he resolved many of his own personal doubts and difficulties while at the same time demonstrating a deep insight into some of the defects of our society and our political structure.

Another question to try to get right is posed by David's poems. From an early age, he wrote poems as a way of expressing his inmost feelings. They were very important to him and at the age of seventeen or eighteen he copied them carefully into three volumes, adding a few compositions later as he wrote them. Later still, he went through them all, making notes on what many of the poems meant to him. He stopped writing regularly in this form when he left school, though his first year at Birmingham University yielded a few more. Last of all, he found release from the war in the South Atlantic through poetry.

How much of all this effort should be included? If one is making a literary judgement, then most of Dave's poems are experiments, early attempts at communication (whether with himself or others) at some level of meaning. As poetry, much of this is interesting but not sufficiently developed to look convincing if printed. Yet these poems do help us to understand the David who was too reticent to open up fully to his parents or to most of his friends. There is a pervasive mood of sadness: how far is this indicative of the real David or (to put it crudely) just part of growing up? The poems which have been included here seem to mark turning points in his life. To some he attached special importance, as evidenced by his notes. The reader who wants to understand David better will want to understand them.

The majority of the poems have not, rightly or wrongly, been given a place. Although David's fate was similar to that of Wilfred Owen – who also died, just as pointlessly, in the final days of a war – it is not claimed that he was another Owen (though he admired Owen's work tremendously). I would gladly be told I am wrong!

In the pages that follow, as far as possible, David is left to tell his story in his own way. The different phases of his life are introduced by narrative sections which have been kept as brief as can be. The first narrative, introducing his childhood and years at school, has to be longer than the rest. David did not leave home, except occasionally, during these years so there are few letters. It is necessary for another to describe these years (which in total form two-thirds of his brief life). Even then, David was making his own strikingly personal comments: as the pages after the initial narrative will prove.

From the many letters of condolence we have received it is clear that David made a strong impression on those who came to know him. Yet it is hoped that this book will also have a message for others. Far away from his homeland, in 1982 one junior Naval officer spoke with the voice of sanity when almost all the eminent, and those who take it on themselves to pronounce on public matters, seem (temporarily, let us hope) to have lost all sense of reality, all sense of proportion, and all thought for the future in the South Atlantic. What David has to say may not be popular with them in the immediate aftermath of the conflict. And in ten years' time his analysis will have been buried in history when the politicians have cobbled up shabby solutions for their sorry errors of judgement. David had to die because of crass error, and weakness disguised as boldness in high places. He died, but he lives in our hearts, and it is possible he may live through these his writings: casual, unintended for publication as they were.

This book is dedicated to Christine: a widow after two years of marriage. It is really also dedicated to the other young widows whose drawn, white faces made one's heart ache at the inspiring *Glamorgan* service of remembrance, held in Portsmouth dockyard on 16 July 1982, as well as to all the others who mourn for the fallen.

Fifteen years ago I dedicated a little book to David and inscribed under his name a thought about experiencing events of the past and the future:

> And some are sung, and that was yesterday,
> And some unsung, and that may be tomorrow.

David's tomorrow was all too brief. So it was for the other young sailors, soldiers and airmen who laid down their lives in the Falklands.

## WE WILL REMEMBER THEM

## Contents

## Illustrations

# 1

## Childhood and School, 1957-1975

David was born on 14 March 1957 soon after midday. His mother went into the maternity hospital at Barnet that morning, and there was time to see our eldest boy, Jonathan, off to school. The birth was, Elisabeth said, an easy one. When I went to see them that evening, David was lying beside her, his skin smooth – not wrinkled – and pink – not red. He seemed to smile through his tranquil sleep. I could not resist picking him up, but though awakened he was not disturbed.

We gave him my names, but for his first name we chose the name of my mentor and benefactor at Cambridge (David Thomson) which was also a name that had recurred among my forbears: David Tinker, born 1861, David Tinker, born 1817, and David Tinker, born 1777. Nine days later they were allowed to leave the hospital. Both Jonathan (then aged 6) and Mark (then aged 4) remember standing at the foot of the hospital staircase, looking up at their Mummy and their new brother. I well remember their wondering little faces. We were all so happy.

David, the baby, was spoilt, He was slow in walking, in talking, and later in reading. Why should he take the trouble? His mother and brothers were only too happy to do things for him. When he was four, we left Barnet for Mill Hill: it was arranged that our sons would later go to school there. David did not like the move. One day, soon after, I went back to our old house (still unsold!), taking David. He was reluctant to come away from the old Victorian house with its rambling garden. Already he showed that strong attachment to *places* which was to be such a feature of his life, culminating in his love affair with the cottage at Clungunford.

Just before he was five, in January 1962, David started going to St Paul's primary school on the Ridgeway at Mill Hill. It was a small, old fashioned school with kindly teachers. Towards the end of his time there, David was able to go to school and return across the fields of Arrandene by himself: a

daily journey which was to become a vital part of his con-
sciousness. We still have some of his early childish compositions.

*18 September 1964*
### My Mummy

My Mummy is always reading to me when I am ill, or plays
games with me in her spare time. Mummy is always ready to
play a game when I come home from school until she has to
get the tea.

*1 November 1964*
### Cycling

I usually go round the block. It is better than sitting indoors
doing nothing. I go lovely and fast. I go about fifteen miles
per hour. But I do not spend all my time out of doors. Because
I get bored of staying out. So I come home and play with
some Airfix soldiers.

*6 July 1965*
### How I Like to Spend my Spare Time

I like to spend my spare time pouring out my collection [of
coins]. I love to do this best, but I don't do this too much
now, because Daddy does not like it now, it gets on his nerves.
When I come home from school I play a game, or sometimes
I hop on to my bed and read. Sometimes, a huge book which
has 487 pages, of which I have only read 228 pages. But
sometimes I read aged, aged, comics, of which most have
been destroyed.

*       *       *

This is the first reference to David's collection, then mostly
Victorian coins received in change, and kept in an old sweets
bottle. (I am sorry I seem to have been so irritable about his
habit of suddenly pouring them out on the table.) In the
following years, the collection became a systematic hobby.
David bought books about coins, and kept the increasing
numbers in albums. Every Saturday morning he and I went
over to Edgware, to an open market where there was a coin
stall. After very careful deliberation he would choose a few
coins: always British or British Empire, he was not interested

in foreign coins. When I brought him back an ancient coin from Rome he was polite, but not really excited.

In the autumn of 1965, David moved on to Hendon Prep School where his brothers had been. This was another old-fashioned school where *learning* was highly valued. Among the masters was a young Welshman, Taff Hill, who influenced David towards expressing himself in language, and an older man "The Major", who encouraged him to think of joining the armed services. David much enjoyed the "Biggles" books and had a large collection of the works of Captain Johns (to whom he successfully appealed for his autograph). The Major encouraged him to think of flying as a career, and addressed letters to "Wing Commander Tinker".

During these years the whole rhythm of our life was changed when I bought our cottage, Aspen Lea, at Little Hampden; small, one-floored, hidden away among the woods and fields of the Chilterns. My feeling about the cottage amounted to a passion, and we had to go down there every weekend, fair or foul, and spend the school holidays there. The boys somewhat resented being taken away from their Mill Hill friends but grudgingly, perhaps, they yielded to the fascination of the rounded hills and the beech woods. They say the Romans never penetrated into the heart of the Chilterns, and although only thirty miles from London, the Chilterns in their inner fastnesses are remote, timeless.

For me, the happiest part of the year was the long summer holidays, when the wood pigeons cooed their reflective note in the tall trees around us, and in the long, long evenings our surrounding trees slowly turned from shades of green to merge in the black of night.

I was absorbed in writing but the boys played, read their books, and went on expeditions. We often went to the Thames-side towns of Wallingford, Abingdon and Goring to take out a skiff for a leisurely afternoon. Elisabeth (whose main joy was to make her boys happy) took them over to Chesham for afternoon visits to the cinema. And in later years the boys and I walked quiet, unfrequented stretches of the Icknield Way: that ancient track of ancient Britain. Every year we had a special walk, when we covered about twenty miles of the old road, never meeting a soul, until at our journey's end was Elisabeth, with the car and a very welcome picnic tea.

Each Sunday we went up to Great Hampden church for
morning service, and after about a year the Rector, Mr Hill,
asked Jonathan and Mark to sing in the choir. Later – one,
two years? – David joined his brothers. He was still quite little,
and there wasn't a surplice and cassock that would fit him;
but there he was, up in the chancel. As they moved towards
the altar before the service, Jonathan walked with an erect,
austere tread: anticipating the priest he was to become. Mark
ambled along, amiably. David trundled forward with a dis-
tinctly nautical roll. Responsive to his surroundings, but not
subdued by them; as he would ever be.

In the autumn of 1970, David went on to Mill Hill School.
In thinking about his life we need to remember that of the
twenty-five years he was allowed in this world, thirteen were
spent at school. They were important in his development; and
the Mill Hill years were specially important.

My choice of this school was conditioned by my own early
experiences. My parents, who were not well-off, strained their
resources to send me to boarding school to give me the best
education they could. Taunton School, where I went, had
some excellent masters (notably those teaching English and
History) but living conditions were crude. Soon after my
arrival a new headmaster placed an absurd over-emphasis
upon games and discipline and devalued scholarship. I too
wanted my boys to have a good education: but not to endure
a games regime or to live away from home. Mill Hill seemed
to supply what I was looking for; then a relatively small school,
there was a tradition of 'liberal' education with a high standard
in choral and orchestral music. Numbers of day boys were
small (only about 30-40) and entry was difficult. The headmaster favoured the sons of professional people – doctors,
ministers, lawyers; so as a professor I found favour in his eyes.
Jonathan and Mark both seemed to appreciate a situation in
which they could always return to the quietness and security
of home while – as school was only ten minutes away, over the
fields – they could stay on for after-school activities if they
desired. I am not at all sure that David appreciated this
arrangement.

The autumn when he went to Mill Hill School saw considerable changes in our home life. Jonathan had gone to university
in 1969 and now Mark also went off to college. For most of the

year, David was virtually an only child. Also, I had become Director of the Institute of Race Relations and was preoccupied with its problems. Elisabeth was left to provide the home life: which she did, with her usual loving care. But David was growing up; their relationship lost something of its old happy intimacy.

To all outward appearances, Dave was the typical school-boy: untidy in his dress, cheerful, casual. Yet he was undergoing inward experiences of which we knew nothing. At Hendon Prep, Taff Hill had encouraged David to express himself by writing poems. Now, spontaneously, all on his own, David was writing away. He hardly ever tried to compose rhyme. All his poems were written in uneven lines of blank verse in which the metre is slow and sometimes jerky. During the summer holiday of 1971 he composed fourteen poems, while twenty-seven more poems were finished by the end of the year. Some are about friendships, with other boys and with girls (or a girl) and they seem to have a charming though callow romantic, melancholic quality. Several are evocations of the places he liked and loved. The physical surroundings of Mill Hill School – rural, pastoral even, amid the bustle of an outer London suburb – affected him deeply. Little Hampden, and its fieldpaths, and tracks through the woods, stirred his sense of history and of country. His poems seem an extension of his own simple observation of his surroundings. Here are some impressions jotted down at our cottage while he was at the same time composing a poem "On Visiting Little Hampden Churchyard":

> And now at the end of an afternoon. A trail of smoke from a cottage chimney rises, accompanied by the lazy sound of an aeroplane drifting across the sky.* The tall, powerful trees stand next to me, their green leaves shading a cooing pigeon, and then with a flapping of wings another settles down to rest. And the birds sing the last songs of the afternoon and the sun slowly descends and I lean back and listen to the sounds of the birds as they herald the end of a day – of eating, living, for the end of one life – and sleeping, for the beginning of another.

*    *    *

* This relates not to the jets which make the skies of the Home Counties hideous but to the old biplanes which members of flying clubs used to take up. We would remark "There goes Biggles" to David's amusement.

One theme is introduced that was to become dominant in David's inward life: that of the Great War, the first world war. As a tiny boy, David had been fond of dressing up in my old army cap and revolver holster, water bottle, and other equipment (just as *I* had spent hours dressing up in *my* father's Great War uniform). But he was never specially interested in the war in which his father and mother had been involved. It was the Great War which haunted him. In his bedroom he pinned up an old map of the Western Front which had belonged to my father's mother. He subscribed to a weekly series, *The Great War*, and he constantly read the works of the Great War poets – Rupert Brooke first, then Siegfried Sassoon, then, for a time, Isaac Rosenberg. But always he returned to Wilfred Owen. He applauded Owen's rejection of all the *bullshit* aspects of war. He cherished Owen's longing for peace instead of war. And in his own writing – whether or not he consciously took Owen as his model – he adopted the same bleak, spare, stripped-down mode of expression. Here is one such offering, written after Remembrance Sunday 1971, when David stood in the uniform of the CCF (the school training corps) in front of the Gate of Honour erected in memory of the school's fallen old boys. Did the ceremonial, the sound of the bugle, provide the atmosphere of tribute?

> Not that – but just those two bare minutes
> When those grey lifeless forms seem to rise up and fight
> For peace – until the Last Post sends them back

David, of course, had few direct contacts with those who fought in the Great War. His grandfather died when David was six: and in any case he never talked about his experiences which, as a Prisoner of War, had ended in nightmare. We gave Dave some of my father's possessions associated with the war, including a Russian soldier's cooking pot in which my father had warmed up the cabbage stalks or whatever it was he had to eat. David burnished the copper till it shone like gold. Among those who attended Great Hampden church were two old men who had been in the trenches – Mr Croft and Mr Bennett. David listened to their stories attentively. But in the main his poetic evocation of the Great War was an act of imagination. All this – or almost all – constituted David's secret life. Outwardly, he was a genial, gregarious schoolboy.

In the autumn of 1971, feeling frustrated with the growing divisions at the Institute of Race Relations, I determined to go off to Mauritius for three weeks to undertake research. We arranged for David to be a temporary boarder in School House. When we returned he did not want to revert to being a day boy, and stayed in School House till the end of term. David commemorated this experience in a poem, written on 8 December 1971:

> There'll always be that early quiet swell
> When even silence hums at six o'clock
> But I shall not be there to see and hear
> The old brick building wake, and meet another day
>
> Tomorrow morning will be running streams and
>     wet green grass
> The old trees nodding off to sleep
> A sense of trying to get back into time
> – Running to school at nine o'clock

David called this poem "Life always goes on"; which wry philosophy became the basis of his attitude to the ups and downs he experienced.

The year 1972 was, for me, one of almost incessant conflict at the Institute of Race Relations. There was an open confrontation in April. Jonathan and Mark were wholehearted in their support of my position, but David found it all rather incomprehensible (he wasn't the only one). About this time, he said to me: "James Baldwin asserts that no black man will ever get a fair trial from a white jury. Is that right?" I replied, "Well, what is important is that black people *think* they can never get a fair trial." David observed: "That's not a straight answer."

Anyhow, it all seemed to end in a victory for the liberal position; but the feuding went on, and in November I decided to quit. Elisabeth and I received an invitation to spend four or five weeks at the Rockefeller Centre in the Villa Serbelloni at Bellagio. David gladly went back to being a boarder again, but this time the experience was not commemorated in a poem. It would seem that he was absorbed in a relationship with a girl, 'B' (quite unknown to us) and this gave more pain than pleasure. The relationship seems to have ended in July 1973 according to a bleak little poem:

A lot of good,
A lot of bad,
A lot was fun,
A lot was sad,
And there was happiness
But now just loneliness

Probably we could not have entered into David's unhappiness by any means; but we simply did not know.

As it happened, that was a very happy summer for me. The Institute was left behind and I was writing the first draft of my book *Separate and Unequal*. We spent a long summer at the cottage. I would write all day and then go for a leisurely walk in the evening. David *seemed* content enough. It was that summer that he decided to dig an enormous hole in the garden. The day began with him raising the Union Jack on a flagpole we had put up in the garden at the back. Then down the hole he would descend, digging deeper and deeper, emerging only for meals. When the sun set, the flag would be lowered. So the summer went on, uneventfully, with David going off for a few weeks to join Mark in the school he and some Cambridge friends organised for gypsy children.

For some time, David had talked about going into the Navy. We encouraged him. It is not quite clear how far this represented a commitment to a life at sea in a fighting service or just a wish for early independence, avoiding the long years at university which both his brothers had entered upon by nature of their chosen vocations. David seemed just right for the Navy: alert, eager, observant. He went down to Portsmouth to take part in officer selection tests (these always have to include a group building an imaginary bridge over an imaginary river). He was successful, and was awarded a Royal Navy Scholarship in October 1973. This guaranteed him a place at Dartmouth in two years' time and meanwhile provided financial assistance with his education. We were delighted, and David seemed pleased and proud.

He was now in the Lower Sixth, and was working hard; though he liked to give the impression that he was taking things easy. His notebooks are set out logically, tidily, systematically. One master recalls his "passion for order and meticulous recording". In his relations with masters, some found him attractive (one speaks of "his moral courage and the cheerful but earnest way he set about his tasks") but others clearly thought him (in Dave's own words) "a pain". He was so direct and uncompromising, and made it very clear when he considered a person didn't know what he was talking about. In the Spring of 1974 David came back one day and gruffly told his mother that he had won the Literary Prize for some poems. She, of course, asked to see them and he gave her some typewritten sheets, observing "You can keep them if you want to". We thought they were very good: of course. But so far as we knew this was an isolated effort. David's main interest seemed to be the Shooting Team. Like all our family, Dave was not much good at ball-games but his eye for shooting was excellent. He often went down to Bisley and perhaps found in its rather primitive, old-fashioned buildings and firing ranges echoes of the days of 1914.

In the summer of 1974 David went to Dartmouth for a spell to get acquainted with the college and its methods. The training ship took them round from London. Dave had to join the ship at the jetty in front of the Tower. We warned him to leave plenty of time, but there was a lot to do and he arrived at the Tower tube station just when the ship was due to leave. Racing to the jetty he saw a boat pulling away. A sailor called "Are you for Dartmouth?". David indicated he was. "Jump" said the sailor. Throwing his bag on board, David jumped. He returned, cheery as ever. If he found some aspects of the Dartmouth system repellent (as he certainly did, one year later) he did not reveal this.

So he came to his last year at school. Unfortunately, the headmaster he had admired and liked departed; and he did not take to the new man. Similarly, the genial and slightly eccentric music master left under uncertain circumstances and the choral music which was such a delight at Mill Hill languished. David was made a house prefect, but soon after he asked to give it up. He pleaded the need to work, but it was really a distaste for what he saw as an unnecessary insistence on authority. This view did not stand in the way of his becoming the head of the school corps; or rather, as an under-officer, its sergeant-major. He was also Captain of shooting and was very proud of the colours blazer he was awarded. Additionally, he was joint editor of the school magazine. The magazine was beautifully set up and printed by an Old Millhillian, who wrote of David: "Although then only seventeen or eighteen he struck me very forcibly as a boy destined for great things. I liked him instantly for in him one could see very much the finer side of English youth." In truth, Dave was very sensitive to the nuances of relationships. He responded warmly to someone sympathetic and he became aloof, even huffy, with a person he found uncongenial.

All went well. David secured the necessary academic qualifications for Dartmouth. He received an award to enable him to travel during the interval between school and Dartmouth. He should have been happy: but was he? He recorded his feelings after the prizes had been awarded on the school's Foundation Day:

> Saturday night on my last Foundation Day, and a mixture of feelings. Already people will have been going to bed and putting this Saturday behind them. But this Saturday night is such a break with the past.
>
> Today is a mixture of Jim Fields, Tim Poole and Humphrey Bangham, all of whom I may not see again. It's a mixture of all the people that I've said goodbye to. All the faces that I started to meet from the time of the scholarship exam in 1970 are now gone. Stephen Briggs, Anthony Marris, both of them seen on the first and last days of Mill Hill. Farewell – Arrandene, chapel, tradition, security.
>
> What lies ahead is violence, Dartmouth, hostility, all the old world left behind and moving on without me. I fear for the future.
>
> The only remedy is to seek peace in the tying-up of security that will exist for evermore in Foundation Day here at Mill Hill, in continuance of friendships made at Mill Hill and in the large possibility of seeing other friends. Secondly, to realise that one has become a first-year again. No responsibility . . . . There will be no hang-ups for the CCF. Take the buffets with stoicism. Do not live a lie. Conform as much as possible, but do not pretend. Follow up the things you are actually interested in . . . .

It seems strange when, to outward appearances, Dave was glad to leave a school with which he had become impatient, with its regulations and restrictions. This was also a time when David had found new friends in the family that had come to the big house nearest to our cottage. They took him in and introduced him to their young relatives and to their friends.

When not with them, David could go for long walks along abandoned railway lines, which he enjoyed; and there was his trip up to Orkney and Shetland – a long train journey, which he liked, and a sea voyage. He seemed happy with his parents – closer to them than he had been in recent years – and when at last the day came for him to go off to Dartmouth he left them at the station feeling that a great adventure was opening up. Perhaps, at this time, David did not really understand himself. One thing which the Navy did for him was to provide a challenge through which he did come to know himself.

## Letters and Poems

*To Granny*                    LITTLE HAMPDEN, *Summer 1965?*

I thank you very much for the very exciting book. I am writing this letter in the corn field next to our swing and I can hear the wheat popping. It is a gorgeous day. It was about medium this morning, a bit hotter and now (in the afternoon) it has become quite hot.

This week we went on the steamer from Wallingford to Goring. It was a good trip, but for the last half hour a wind sprang up and it was quite cold after that, but it was not too bad, and we got off and went home.

*To Granny*                    LITTLE HAMPDEN, *August 1966*

I am sorry to hear that you are not feeling well. I hope you will be better soon. We have had Jonathan's GCE results and they are excellent! He passed in all seven [subjects] that he took.

Another thing.

When we were out on a walk, a day when Jonathan was away in Malta, we came across a caravan [used long ago by a shepherd] which had a ladder in it. Mark would not let me have the ladder. I pointed out to him that the ladder would not be used again in its lifetime as the caravan was deserted.

I have had my school report now and I will tell you the things in order of bestness: History, 94, 1st, English, 88, 1st [etc.] . . . .

And now a very sad thing.

Nip [our cat] attacked a baby rabbit this morning (Tuesday) and we rushed to the scene but Nip had killed the rabbit by then. As a punishment he did not have any dinner at all.

Well, Goodbye for now, and I hope that you will get better. By the way, I'm sending my report with this letter, so Goodbye for now. Goodbye.

HENDON PREP SCHOOL, *Spring 1970*

*Paradoxy (Extracts)*

Do not the winged squadrons of the sky
Pour down bombs upon this wretched earth?
Does not a bloody mass of child
Cause God to erupt in silent wrath?

Does not the dawn bring death
To yet another one?
Is not there one more angel to replace
The one that fell, wounded, wingless to the ground?

Is not God happy when a soldier
Fights for his own blood-thirsty country?
Does not his wrath open up
When this soldier is killed by another?

Does not the soldier in the mud and the blood
Think of the green fields beyond?
Themselves to be turned
To the mud and the blood?

Dulce et decorum est pro patria mori
Those words were not on their lips as they died.
They did not die in the green fields
But in the mud and blood of the trenches

The darkened skies of man
Where angels fear to tread
Can God's power override
The Devil with a gun?

[David was asked to be editor of a literary and social magazine for Hendon Prep. He wrote about half of the mag himself! This poem as printed is much longer, and the strength of its feeling is greater than its literary skill. The reference to "the mud and the blood" and "the green fields" almost certainly relate to the colours borne by the Motor Machine Guns, later Royal Tank Corps, in which my father served in the Great War: brown, red, green: supposedly they mean "Through the mud, through the blood, to the green fields beyond". Michael (Taff) Hill helped Dave with this mag and wrote this character-sketch of him: "Dreamer, man of letters and playground lout, David has emerged from his fantasy world to edit this magazine. Eyes still a little creased from looking down hot gun barrels . . . he has directed us all with verve and enthusiasm. But as a writer – watch this name in future."]

HAMPDEN, BUCKS, *21 August 1971*

*Monument*

Watching birds circle and wheel in your mist-enshrouded
    valley
You've watched the seasons change and go
The harvest ripened, reaped and stored
And all along you've just been waiting, patiently
Some day, perhaps, there'll come along another
To knock you down and put you somewhere else
But when you've gone there'll still be that silent freedom
Of beauty, fading into morning mist

[Against this poem, David just wrote "The John Hampden Monument". This simple memorial stands by the roadside, amid the Hampden woods, looking across to our own fields and trees. We took walks which led us past the memorial hundreds of times over the years. There is a sense of space and stillness and timelessness about the place, which David's little poem evokes.]

MILL HILL SCHOOL, *15 September 1971*

*The Evening Before the Start of the Autumn Term*

You're so quiet:
Have you awakened yet?
Even with the blazing House lights
And new boys walking expectantly round the place
You're still asleep,
Still holding on,
Still sheltering in the pungent shadows of the past
Still lingering on – They darkly fill
The single soundless corridor
Of old bedraggled Murray House.
And there you lie
By tall dark silent trees
And you can dream forever
Of hot cricket days
Of April showers
Of nightingales in June –
And you can sleep
Till wakened by our shouts
Of "Come on Blues"
That raise you, bleary-eyed from rest
To shed your Autumn leaves
And wait for Spring

*To H and E*          SCHOOL HOUSE, MILL HILL SCHOOL,
                                         *26 November 1971*

Despite a wet and mild November, the snow starts to fall as masters work themselves up into a state of frenzy for exams, notably Froggy Brown, whose latest antic is crawling round the floor pretending to be Hugh Gueslin.*

At the beginning of a Physics lesson we are standing in the main lobby of the Science Block, waiting for permission to go into a Lab. Powney (our Physics master) comes out and says "Room 14, Mr Knowles". So we go to have a lesson with Goofy Knowles. After about ten minutes of this, Powney comes back in again and says "I do not recall telling you to come in here. If you do not want to come to my lesson you can go and stand in the middle of the Quadrangle". So we march en masse into the middle of the Quad and stand there, eating, cracking jokes, when Powney comes after about ten minutes again and tells us to come in. Nobody knows whether he said "If" or "Since", but we ended up doing a two page essay
. . . .

What I really wanted to write to you about was about staying on in School House until the end of term. The fun really starts in the last week, and at present that's when I'm leaving. If it's all right by you I can ask the Robot [house master] and get it fixed. There isn't much point in only staying in School House for the weeks when nothing happens and then when it livens up, push off . . . .

Once you start boarding, the time between weeks is just irrelevant. The only measurements you can use are half terms. Being a day boy isn't anything like boarding. You miss so much of the GC life on a 9-5 day.†

By the way, Dixon's back [on TV].

* Gueslin: a character in a French set book.
† GC = Games Committee, a term for the social life of the school.

MILL HILL SCHOOL, *17 December 1971*

*Old Murray House: After a Term of Desolation*

You're still here
And time encloses you again
In ever-growing grass and springing weeds
And still through time you stumble on
As though t'were Spring and Summer
All those months you've lost
And all those people gone.
Stripped of your rank
You can't pretend to be
Old Murray House, the Rifle Range,
Or any other thing, but what you are:
A beautiful old building, just with memories
For us, the last of those you knew

[The "House" the Mill Hill day boys had was really rather an odd erection, standing apart from the main buildings. During David's time at school the day boys moved into new accommodation, and old Murray was abandoned. David wrote against this piece: "I regarded this as one of the most beautiful things I had written. If you forget the clichés it still is quite enjoyable. It is poignant for me, anyway. I wrote it in Murray House after the end of term and I can still remember the freshness of that morning, and the peculiar smell of burnt paper that used to characterise Old Murray"].

*To H and E*                    ROUEN, *14 March 1972*

A rather inappropriate postcard I'm afraid,* but I had to change a 10 Franc note in a hurry.

Things have been going well here. I stay with two families, one [during the] week, t'other weekends. A hectic day in Paris yesterday with a family who are backseat drivers with a tendency to scream. If they spoke a placid language like English they wouldn't get so hysterical. The other family live in a chateau the other side of Rouen with everything out of the best film sets. On returning [to London] transport has been arranged and I will be arriving Saturday night or Sunday morning.

* The Bayeux Tapestry, showing Norman cavalry in pursuit of Harold's men.


MILL HILL, *12 March 1973*

*Sonnet: At the Reverberations Upon Whistling Elgar at Night*

Why do you wake the children from their sleep
As they lie in time-old cots in upper rooms?
Why make them listen from the dark?
As you whistle on your way to school
Why do you whistle louder still
And drown your song in endless wail?
Why wake the children from the past?
Their grown-up forms have left them long ago

These strains remember childhood long ago
I wake them so they may not lose
Those watchful moments, wakened from half sleep
So when they too have grown, they too
May not forget the whistling from a Summer night
Because they never woke my childhood from the dead

[This poem seems to evoke some memory from early child-hood. "Time-old cots": David inherited the cot used by his brothers, and already old when he slept in it. "Whistling Elgar": Dave's great love from an early age: is this a reference to the last theme in the *Enigma Variations* where the composer is whistling, signalling to his wife, "I'm home"? David just noted against this poem: "I find a sense, a great sense of profundity by whistling at night down suburban roads".]


*To H and E*                                    WISBECH, *28 August 1973*

Considering your plans for Saturday, 2nd September, I have come up with a good idea. In Wisbech is a marvellous old house, Peckover House, which stands on the North Brink. I feel sure you would enjoy a visit there. The house, as such, is fairly interesting; it has four well furnished rooms with a library (unfortunately devoid of books) on the ground floor. The rooms do not have ungainly ropes around them and look better for it.

However, the gardens are magnificent. They are not well laid out but are like a series of cottage gardens, with an old high wall round the edge, and a long-haired black cat. The gardens contain everything from orange trees to palm trees and 14th Century barns. You will really like it: mainly because it won't be flooded with tourists. It opens at 2 p.m. and one could *easily* spend two hours there . . . . It's an idea, but of course isn't compulsory.

[David had gone to Wisbech to join a summer school which Mark had organised for the children of travellers (gypsies). As a centre of fruit and vegetable growing, Wisbech employs the travellers as harvesters. Mark reported that though David had not met the travellers before he immediately established a rapport with them and with their children. Of course we paid a visit to Peckover House. We found that David was on good terms with its custodian, and the gardens had for us the magical quality which he had discovered.]

MILL HILL, *27 March 1974*

*Souvenirs of Mill Hill School*

*To School, over Arrandene in the Morning*

I walked across Arrandene this morning
And absent-mindedly ate a leaf
Off some bush that was trying to grow
In the hedgerow.
I was very surprised
It didn't taste of car fumes
Or industrial waste or
Detergent foam.
It just tasted of
leaf.
So I ate another
And that too surprised me.
There was only a trace of carbon-monoxide
    poisoning.
But it *was* early Spring
And the hedgerow was laced with light-green
    trailings
Of opening buds, and the tiny fluffy nettles
Had just come through the dusty brown layers
Of dead leaves, and the willow tree
Was starting to trail its endless green fronds
Over Wells Field –
So I'll give it some time
To mature and grow dulled,
And I'm sure I'll find that
This bush will produce
Leaves to my taste

*On Seeing the Quoted Inscription in an Old Book Written*
*About the Holy Roman Empire in the School Library*

"Since the writing of this book,
The League of Nations has been joined".
Poor fool, he didn't know
That Charles the Fifth's vain efforts
To unite the world

Were just as laughable
As Wilson's efforts to bring true his dream.
I could have added:
"Another war that ravished Europe
Was of this Convention born".
I would not have written:
"Once more, the world has tried
To bring peace through the UNO"
No; not wise after the event,
Nor even cynical of the Twenties' hopes –
But disillusioned with the past
So that the future will not fail me.


*The Effects of a Lower Sixth Arts Course*

They used to say
That all the bad people went to Hell
And all the good people went to Heaven,
But that was getting harder to accept each year
So, by the Fifth Form everything was
Re-incarnation, spirits, mediums.
But in the Lower Sixth
Heaven and Hell is out
And only the Chaplain seems to hold with God
And even then, you have to take the Bible with a
     pinch of salt.
"It's all in the mind", they say,
"The Victorians invented life after death,
You're just a human, acting by instinct".
"Then why do we go to chapel?",
Nobody sings
Oh . . .
Religion is really complicated in the Lower Sixth

*Midday Choir Practice: the Mystical Strangeness of the Music School**

And Fields was blowing down a clarinet reed
And the sun sinked slowly into the black thick polish
Of the Music School floor
And the chairs were banging
And the central doors were open against
    the cold plaster walls
And Fields blew into a trumpet mouthpiece
And the music master was trying to start
    a choir practice
and he gazed down at the piano
And nobody had turned up
And Fields was blowing down his trumpet
    mouthpiece

* David noted that this piece was written three weeks earlier (5 March)
than the others in this sextet: three lines which evoke Autumn (and
seem out of place) have been omitted.


*A Shooting Match: Masters v. School, 25 March 1974*

We had a masters' shooting match yesterday
And they weren't much good –
The rifles didn't seem to fit them
And they couldn't get their eyes behind the
backsight
TC put his glasses on and the lenses fell out
RD said in his Irish lilt:
"Would you mind turnin' the radiator off me?
It's meltin' me feet".
Briggs shot for us.
He had ten shots
He missed six times.
They rigged the competition
They had eight each – we only had five.
Apart from Briggs,
RD lost his.
We had a masters' shooting match yesterday.

*From School: End of the Day: homewards across Arrandene
in the Evening*

The light had not quite gone
For I could still see the dull holes
Of puddles in the fields before me
And all the trees were swaying slightly
But the wind was quiet
And it bore up the stream of the traffic
From out beyond the hill
Like some quiet, flowing, waterfall
As its sound rises away
And the three poplars far away
Were erect and motionless and seemingly dead.
But the clattery thorn bush behind me
Brought the cold of the evening on
And the colourless red sky
Dropped to a colourless black
And the birdsongs were dead
But the traffic streamed on

[This group of poems earned David the Old Millhillians'
Literary Prize: the adjudicator noted their "careful observation, sincerity of feeling and, above all, absence of pretentious-
ness".]

*To H and E* B̶RITANNIA ROYAL NAVAL COLLEGE, DARTMOUTH,
*7 August 1974*

End of the first week.* And two hours free. The only adverse thing about BRNC is that there is no time to enjoy the excellent food (i.e. ten minutes per meal). Nevertheless, now I have got into the routine here it is quite easy to get up for a 6.30 run, even after the night and evening exercise that turned us in about 2 a.m. this morning (Tuesday). I will be in *Birmingham* Division (named after a destroyer) and they are going to put me in to working in the office as well (staff work at an early age . . .) Please send me some MONEY (£1). As I will be in the office it won't be intercepted, but please put the name of my Division on the address. The money has gone on victualling charges and extra rail fares and washing powder, etc (about £2.50). There's no time to buy anything in the NAAFI or enjoy a few pints.

PS.: They make brilliant fudge in Paignton. Shall I bring some?

* David was doing an "acquaint" for those who would be coming to BRNC the following autumn.

*To H and E*                    WALLS, SHETLAND ISLES, *August 1975*

Weather appalling, gusts intolerable, islanders incomprehensible, yet nevertheless some remarkable scenery. The cliffs are quite spectacular. We went to Fair Isle the other day. The seagulls just hover there in the thermals off the cliffs, completely motionless, like bird-men. They look as if they are flying for pure enjoyment.

We are staying in Lerwick for the moment – a grey, sombre, granite town, but the inhabitants seem quite cheery about it.

[In his last term at school, David won a travel grant with another boy to do a "project" on the Orkneys and Shetlands on the eve of the coming of the oil industry. They took a lot of photographs and put in a report. David returned with some splendid kippered haddocks which a fisherman had given him.]

# 2

## First Year in the Navy, 1975-76

David's own account of his time at Dartmouth and on *HMS Intrepid* requires no commentary. This was his first prolonged absence from home and doubtless he looked to us for support. He wrote often, and we replied as often. His account of how the Navy trains its young officers is somewhat alarming, reminiscent in many ways of attitudes of fifty years ago. However, Dave seemed to survive, and indeed thrive. He and his term passed out on 12 April 1976. They marched up the main steps of the college in slow time, swords at the 'present', to the strains of *Auld Lang Syne*: through the great doors, then slamming the doors they gave a great cheer. It was a thrilling moment.

After enjoying leave, David reported to *HMS Fife* at Portsmouth. *Fife* was, and seemingly still is, an unlucky ship, for which nothing goes right. So much time was spent tied up against the dockyard wall at Portsmouth that those responsible for training decided to send Dave and his shipmates under training off to other ships for a brief spell. Dave went to join a minehunter, *HMS Bronington*, then commanded by the Prince of Wales. Within the limits of the little ship, Dave was able to observe his royal Captain closely, and the Prince was kind to his temporary Mid, having friendly conversations with him on the bridge and in the Wardroom. Dave wrote us a long letter about this experience which unfortunately we cannot trace. Probably we showed the letter proudly to all our friends and managed to lose it.

All too soon, Dave returned to *Fife* and the sedentary existence in Portsmouth Dockyard. Finally, in September, before they all went off to universities (or in some cases to the engineering college, Manadon) they returned to Dartmouth for debriefing. Dave was envious of those Mids who had been sent to frigates operating around Iceland in what was the last phase of the Cod War. He had his stories of the time with the Prince: but for the rest, it had been a washout.

And so, with mixed feelings about the Navy, he went off to Birmingham University.

*To H and E* BRITANNIA ROYAL NAVAL COLLEGE, DARTMOUTH,
*1 October 1975*

I'm sorry not to have written before but the NAAFI has only just got a supply of [airmail] paper and envelopes. Thank you for your letters: it has been really good to hear from the outside world and Mauritius seems to be great fun.

Life at Dartmouth is exactly like being a First Year at Mill Hill [School], from sweeping floors and polishing door knobs to filling in Activities Lists. Surprisingly, life is not very hard. Most people arrived having seen the *Panorama* programme on Sandhurst and half were prepared to turn round and go back. But it has not really been like that at all.

EMAs have been exceptionally easy.* The Instructor Lieutenants, aged about twenty-five, and used to armchairs, have tended to keep the pace slow through their utter exhaustion, poor chaps; and so they are really no more than a little jog around the college at five-six m.p.h. Also, for one in every three days we do parade-training EMAs. The standard is fairly low and the G.I.s (Gunnery Instructors, i.e. drill instructors) spend most of the time showing the squad how a movement is done, rather than letting the squad do it. Result: not much progress. Unfortunately their dialogue is rather pathetic. Only the Colour Sergeant, Royal Marines, comes out with amusing phrases, like "You've got the brains of a rocking-horse, Sir", "You horrible little man, Sir". They spend a lot of time giving stick to the graduate entry when they turn Left having been ordered to turn Right, etc.

Off the parade ground, outdoor life has been enjoyable. One spends about six hours or so on the river each week – good weather so far – however, one disastrous incident! I was trying to take a test in a "Bosun" sailing dinghy. Not knowing much about it, I had decided to have a go and unfortunately, instead of having embarked a Mid to act as examiner, I had Lieut. Commander Gedge (one of the Assistant Divisional Officers)

* EMAs = Early Morning Activities.

aboard. I managed to get the thing to move but unfortunately, having staggered fairly unsuccessfully around the course, I set a course across a slack piece of water. No wind, and one big current sweeping us down river. We managed to get alongside another pontoon farther down but unfortunately hit a rather expensive yacht on the way! "I was not impressed, Tinker" was his comment; followed by a five-minute talk on how could I ever expect to be a Naval Officer?

Nevertheless, College life has its uplifting moments as well as its depressing times. Over the weekend we did the "New Entry Exercise" (orienteering with packs), the run-up to Dartmoor. Navigating at the head of my Watch all the way, with people up to eight years older than me, we charged around 30 minutes ahead of everyone else, and without ANY mistakes in navigation.

Also, another morale booster was the swimming test which I managed to pass first time (thank goodness). It was in the first few days before the actual start of term, when I was still feeling comparatively full of energy. The test was four lengths in a boiler suit. When I got to the shallow end I stood on the bottom and had a rest (fortunately, the Petty Officer in charge was giving stick to someone at the other end). Therefore I managed to have enough breath to dive down to retrieve the brick. Also, we didn't have to tread water for three minutes, as stipulated. So – it was a very good piece of fortune. I don't think I would be able to do the test now!

It is amazing how much everything has to be drilled and ordered. We do gym in ranks, and climb ropes or go over the box to drill sequence. Kit, of course, has to be IMMACULATE as the Staff Sergeant PTI would have it. Gym shorts have to have creases, and laces and shoes have to be a brilliant white, although naval-issue shoes have special eyelets which make the laces absolutely black. The kit laid out for inspection (i.e. "Rounds" in the evening) one learns *never* to touch. After you have marked (and how tedious that was – twelve pairs of socks, etc), ironed, and folded kit to the EXACT measurements (my beautifully ironed shirts, half an inch too wide, were thrown out with glee by the Divisional Mid: i.e. Head of House!) *then* you go and buy from Slops all the kit that you are actually going to use. You live out of your laundry box (where clothes have to be folded, but not to exact measurements) or conceal all this clothing in the baggage room. What a farce! But it's the only way to survive. You just don't have time otherwise.

As it is, we go to bed about 12.30 p.m. and get up at 5.45. You are very lucky if you can arrange more than six hours' sleep for yourself. One compensation, however, is that you learn to go to sleep within ten minutes of your head touching the pillow. One previous insomniac described it as pure heaven!

However, Dartmouth is not the absolute hell I thought it would be for the first four weeks. The only thing that is slightly daunting is that they say to you: "To be a Naval Officer you have got to do this, this, and this". All of which seems absolutely awful, as no matter how hard you try you can never please them.

Life as a Middy has its advantages. You feel an almost childish lack of responsibility. They expect you not to be able to close-haul your tie up to your stiff collar, and being treated like a public-school First Year, you behave like one; skiing down the Hawke corridors in your smooth, leather-soled shoes. Another childish aspect is when you march around on Divisions to the accompaniment of a Marines band playing jolly tunes, conducted by an amazing comic-opera band-master with a waxed moustache.

I'll write again soon, when I get some time. Keep the letters coming. It's nice to hear how you are getting on in Mauritius.

*To H and E*                    BRNC, DARTMOUTH, *5 October 1975*

An astonishing event has occurred – a day off [it was Sunday]. With the NEX* last weekend (the orienteering course), today is the first relaxed day that I have experienced at BRNC. Last night I was able to get to bed by 10.30 and I got up today at 8 o'clock. Nine hours' sleep! Life seems much rosier after a good night's sleep. The Navy does not seem so foreboding when you are rested, as when they present it as an uphill grind when your eyelids have extreme difficulty in staying open.

* NEX = New Entry Exercise.

However, the pace of life has considerably slackened. All kit has been marked and now lies untouched in lockers. Boots have now got to the stage where only a few minutes' work will make them gleam. The spate of gym and parade training lessons in weeks 1 and 2 has now dropped, so that we have to present ourselves in "Immaculate" kit less often. Washing does not need to be done more than twice a week. However, Rounds in the evening always presents its little quirks. An Assistant Divisional Officer (ADO) takes Rounds every night and has his own little fetishes. Lieut. Wight spends about five minutes examining the tops of my mess undress shirts (as yet, of course, unused and only ironed). Lieut. Grimes examines the soles of boots at the front (the vertical parts in front of the toe-caps, which being leather have to be polished). The DO, Lieut. Commander Denes examines socks and books (which of course have to be in a straight line at the bottom of the wardrobe to a set pattern). Lieut. Hill, RM of course just examines toe-caps and wouldn't care twopence if the whole dormitory was in a complete mess. The best man to take Rounds is Surgeon Lieut. Commander Evans who whizzes round the whole Division, Standing Rounds, in ten minutes saying "Excellent, excellent. Good Lord, you don't have to fold laundry do you?" (Lieut. Grimes took one hour forty minutes).

With an easing of life we have come to realise that the main upward grind will still be there after the four weeks. It is just the little added extras that won't be there, such as Rounds and EMAs. However, it's quite amusing to note that the punishment "Charlie" routine is really quite a blessing to the new entry. Most of the things entailed are done by us already (EMAs, Rounds, etc.) and the only extra things are musters at meal times: which means you have to move so fast to get to the muster on time that you actually get to the meals.*

Anyway, I have some dates for you. Half Term is Friday 31 October – Monday 3 November. End of Term is Monday 22 December. The last weekend is full of fun, ball, cocktail party, passing out parades, etc.

---

\* From this it seems as though David was himself on the punishment routine.

*To H and E*          BRNC, DARTMOUTH, *15 October 1975*

I hope you are not finding Mill Hill too chilly after the warmth of Mauritius. It seems to have become suddenly colder this week, and press-ups on a wet rugby pitch at 6 a.m. have seemed to lose some of their appeal.

Now, halfway through the fourth week the end is pretty much in sight. However, this week has been really hectic. In the first gym period of the week we were taken by the most hulking ox of a man you could ever imagine with a head like a bull. That hour really was horrific. If anyone moved a muscle out of line the penalty was ten agonisingly slow press-ups for the whole class. Once he bellowed: "What speed do we move at in the gym?" "Full speed, Staff" we replied obediently. "NO", he roared, "We move at TOP SPEED". More press-ups. We had another period of gym today: fortunately it wasn't the ox. I think they must have locked him away back in his padded cell again. I think they only unleash him once on a class!

Last night we had a fire exercise during Rounds. It was up in Hawke, so all the duty parties from the other Divisions had to come charging [up the hill] to Hawke with fire-extinguishers, etc. (poor chaps). Great fun: alarm bells ringing: all super stuff . . . . On another happy note, the Navy have said that I can read History at a university of my choice, which should be just the ticket having had a year in the Navy, to take a few breaths between A Levels and a degree.

I will ring you up on Sunday at 7 p.m. or thereabouts (if the phone is not free). I am afraid that I will reverse the charges because having to buy so much extra kit has left me with 20p. Lastly, can you post me the mess undress black waistcoat and one of my history essays on Cromwell's difficulties in establishing constitutional government (on my desk). Thanks very much.


*To H and E*          BRNC, DARTMOUTH, *26 October 1975*

Thank you very much for sending on the waistcoat, and especially the nice cheque which has solved all my financial straits.

The week has been full of fun, though now slightly tiring. On Tuesday we had the Trafalgar Night Dinner in the Senior Gunroom with the Royal Marines band converting itself into a first class chamber orchestra(!) playing suitable music in the gallery. A really marvellous occasion, made even more magnificent by the fact that this was the first time we had been treated as "Officers and Gentlemen" rather than junior seamen, cleaning the brasses of Hawke Division. Quite an astounding contrast.

On Wednesday I was one of the crew for the weekly interdivisional yacht race (40 ft yachts). A Force 5 wind was blowing – really exciting. We were all sailing at about 15-20 knots in this wind, in addition to plunging through the great sea that was swelling up. It was quite amazing to see the other yachts alongside, coming out of the water about six feet below the waterline and then plunging down, obscured by a wave. Our cox'n had incredible arm ache afterwards, in trying to keep the yacht on a steady course.

Over the weekend we have been on a Divisional exercise, rather like the New Entry Exercise, taking the picket boats up to Teignmouth and then running around on shore playing "Escape and Evasion Exercise", i.e. hide and seek. We were the "hunted". Unfortunately we ran around the course so fast the "hunters" never caught up with us (except for once) and we also lost our accompanying Staff Officer who retired exhausted after the first checkpoint! At one stage we were nearly caught by the hunters so we dived into a nearby wood. Lying prone with head down I automatically went to sleep. When I woke up about ten minutes later I saw all these trees and thought "Good God, where on earth is this?" I'm accustomed to waking up in class rooms and lecture halls but to wake up in a wood was a novel experience.

Now that Week 5 is over we are back to EMAs (guard duty) for the next seven weeks, so it was a short rest for us. Never mind: half term is shining like a beacon above it all (we have been counting the days off since Week 3!) so I look forward to seeing you then. I will arrive 7 p.m. Friday at Great Missenden and leave early after lunch on Monday.

Unfortunately, a sad note to end on. I heard recently that poor old Froggy Brown had died – last Sunday (heart attack). It must have been quite unexpected.

See you Friday.

[I duly met the 7 p.m. train at Missenden. David was not on it, nor on the next one. So I drove back to our cottage, where I found Dave telling salty stories to his mother. He had decided to get off at the previous station down the line, Amersham, and take a taxi. On arriving at the cottage his first words were "I say, can you lend me five pounds?"]


*To H and E*                BRNC, Dartmouth, *8 November 1975*

By now I suppose you are enjoying the comfort of Italy and the Villa Serbelloni. Is that where you have the *chaise longue*? I wonder if we presented the parade Fleet Chief [Petty Officer] with one might it even change his outlook on life?

Thanks for a really marvellous half-term. It really was good to sit around and not be on time for anything. On the train back, everybody admitted they had entertained the idea of not going back at all!

As rather expected, we were greeted with rude shocks. Not content with making us pass the swimming test we now have to pass the bronze "Personal Survival" test: eight times *around* the swimming pool (= 16 lengths). As you can imagine, there is no such word as NO in the RN. You just go round and round until you do it. I was only on lap four when everybody else had finished, so there I was, paddling away on my own. Fortunately it wasn't the ox taking us: he would have probably thrown bricks at me to make me swim faster. However, that's not all; THAT was only a warm-up. The real thing comes on Monday when we wear pyjamas and dive to retrieve two bricks at the deep end.

Having recovered from that rude shock we have been given even more on the parade ground. The parade staff received a rocket for producing a shambolic guard at the beginning of the week. So, as the stable boy kicks the cow, the Midshipman is usually at the end of the kicking line. We doubled up and down the ramps four times before we even got to the parade ground: and when we got there we were met by the Colour Sergeant who greeted us with: "Today is Pain Day". Fortunately, being the crack squad we came off quite well, but grim reminders kept appearing, running past us with rifles over their heads, going up and down the ramps. As you can imagine, the speed of our drill improved considerably. When giving the command "Stand at EASE" our feet were at the correct position by the time he had finished the word EASE (pretty fast). Of course, he still told us that we were bone idle and that when we got to the Fleet we might even have to work an 18-19 hour day, and then we'd really get it in the neck, etc. Unfortunately nobody had the courage to tell him that because he had got us up at 0530 hours to do extra drill we were working an eighteen hour day already.

The new Senior Sub-Lieutenant (= Head of School) is of course very zealous to carry out his duties (being only six weeks at Dartmouth), giving us nice punishments for little things, as is the role of all Senior Mids who want good reports. Thank goodness we are at Hawke. He hasn't got the energy to come steaming up here, so we are comparatively safe most of the time.

This morning (going to Alderney)* we had a super lie in until 0600 hours (it really does make all the difference). Heaving all our copious gear down to *Walkerton* (the mine-sweeper attached to BRNC) we were raring to go. Outside [the Dart] we struck a Force 8. It was really super. I was allowed to play Officer of the Watch, standing (or rather hanging on!) at the front of the bridge, with binoculars, etc. saying "Port, five degrees: Starboard, 1 42", or whatever, and whizzing about plotting fixes (i.e. from bearings on land to get our position at sea). The old minesweeper was doing 30 degree rolls, and plunging in and out of the waves. Imagine my disappointment, leaping from side to side of the bridge, performing Tarzan acts among the voice pipes, (in 30 degree roll) when the Captain says that it's too rough to carry on. My first command in ruins!

It was a bit of a bore, after all the preparation, both of drill and kit, and all the excitement. However, that was that. From the direction of the wind it would have been impossible to dock at Alderney and *Walkerton* might not have survived a passage to Guernsey. So much for the elite guard: not even in the

---

* David's squad had been detailed to provide a guard of honour for Remembrance Day in Alderney.

Dartmouth town guard, nor even BRNC guard, but mere onlookers.

Such is life. Since they started putting the pressure on life has become much more humorous. Dartmouth certainly teaches you to smile in adversity. At the end of the day I feel absolutely elated to have survived it at all! A distinct case of masochism.

Hope you are enjoying a life of ease in Italy.

*To H and E*                    BRNC, DARTMOUTH, *26 November 1975*

In Bellagio you must find it difficult to imagine a situation where a spare hour is a rare thing. I'm happy to say that these are the first two hours "spare" I have been able to get for about two weeks! It has been incredibly hectic here: the first four weeks were really nothing in comparison.

At the same time as the Alderney Guard was washed out, the normal BRNC guard was behaving abominably. Therefore, our class was sent in to bolster them up. However, the guard was still so awful that 6 a.m. EMAs were ordered. So instead of getting up at 0530 hours and yawning, plodding about, getting washed, etc. we had to spring out of our beds and rush around with not a second to spare. On the day when we had to do "air bedding" (folding blankets etc. up into 2 foot squares), as well as put our battledress on, and boots, stiff collars, webbing etc: you have never seen a group of people move so fast. However, on one day when we were scheduled to embark on *HMS Walkerton* at 1710 hours, we had breakfast at 0630, and a lie-in until 0600. "What's half an hour's difference?" you might say: but our joy was heartfelt.

These days (since Monday) in my new life of ease I lie in until 0600 hours and then have time for a bath – in unhurriedness. That *is* luxury.

You may also be surprised to hear that I have passed all my necessary boat tests. On the day I took my dinghy test, guess who was DRO (Duty River Officer)? None other than Lieut. Commander Gedge (of boat-crash fame). Those are the only two times I have ever seen him on the river: but despite this evil omen I still passed.

My picket boat (45 feet) test was a gift from the gods. The PO taking us passed everyone. Normally, Hawke officers taking these tests fail you for microscopic details. My Dory test (v. small speed boat) was also a piece of luck: the only time in the afternoon when I managed to do the manoeuvres properly. When I reported to the DRO for his verdict (he is a real pain as far as river things go) he said: "What mistakes did you make?" I hummed and haa-ed, not really able to think of any. "What mistakes did you make?" he virtually screamed at me, looking as if he would grasp me by the neck and throttle me. "None, consciously, Sir", I replied. "That's right", he said "NONE". My jaw dropped.

Over the weekend we went on a DIVEX (Divisional Exercise) to do a fun orienteering course designed by the Marines (which we nearly won), and some canoeing – also fun. However, it was just so wet and cold, and in sailing back it was also *so* wet that BRNC has never looked so welcoming before. (Dartmoor on 8 December should be just right!)

On the universities front, Cambridge is out, unfortunately. Apparently the Director of Studies only sends the chosen few there and closed his list on 31 September (before we had heard anything about universities). I'm sorry to have put you to the trouble of writing around to no avail, but there it is.* Pipers always play required tunes.

I received some lovely loot from the bank a couple of weeks ago: very useful. The system of pay here is extraordinary. My pay seems to be going down while the tax goes up. This month I was paid (in real money) only £10 more than the tax man took for the last month.

After the next test and Captain's Rounds are over, from the beginning of next week, life will be very rosy indeed. No more tests, no guard duty, no more river tests to get: a life of ease. Next week we go flying for two days, and Week 12 is taken up with preparing for the DTS† (*Intrepid*). We are going to Barbados, St Lucia, and a couple more islands, and then visit Texas for their 200th Anniversary. That should be a run

---

* Sidney Sussex College, Cambridge, had indicated that they would favourably consider David (his brother had been there) but as Dave relates he was not given the option.
† DTS = Dartmouth Training Squadron; at this time actually the assault ship INTREPID so Dartmouth Training Ship.

ashore – and a half ! Gone, now, are the hectic weeks behind. The Mids coming back from the DTS were absolutely shocked when they arrived. It was never like this last term: we don't even get gym next week.

I hope you are both keeping well: thanks for your letters. I hope the remainder of your stay will be enjoyable.

*To H and E*                    BRNC, DARTMOUTH, *4 December 1975*

Had a great day today: we went flying in a Wasp [helicopter]. It was marvellous to see Dartmouth from the air: it looked really pleasant. All the hills we struggled up on NEX looked utterly gentle and peaceful. A BR train chuffed by on the old GWR line, just like a toy train set. It was amazing just to take off from a football field and motor on up into the sky. At 1200 feet on our approach landing, the pilot decided to do the famous "drop", when the engine is switched off and you are prevented from crashing into the ground by changing the pitch of the rotor blades and getting lift from them at just 15 feet above the ground. From 1200 to 15 feet they're just whirling around flat, so as to preserve momentum but not giving lift: because to prolong lift the blades slow down rapidly.

Anyway, at 1200 feet he switched off the engine. I took a deep breath, and we plummeted down. For the first five or seven seconds it was a hairy feeling, as the nice reassuring lift I was feeling from the floor of the Wasp stopped and we just fell, as the forward speed was converted to downward speed. However, once we were all falling at the speed of gravity there wasn't a sickening downward force. The skill with which the pilot prevented the Wasp from obliterating itself (and us) was consummate.

In the afternoon we did a navigational exercise. I was very surprised when we actually arrived at this obscure village having steered the course I calculated! . . .

This evening also brought an entertaining incident. As you know, BRNC is hierarchical, so that you have to call Mids a year older "Sir". Tonight I was first Duty Mid, and one of the tasks is to collect leave cards at 2230 hours from Main Office (down hill and back again). A strict rule prevents ringing up the office first to find if there are any cards there. However, I did ring up, giving name of Division, etc. It was [answered by] OOW1 (Officer of the Watch, 1) a very big gun indeed. During the course of my asking if there were any leave cards there I suddenly realised he was calling me "Sir". Not wishing to give him any doubts as to his conviction [of superior rank] I put on my best public school voice and asked him to find out if there were leave cards present. He replied that there were: "Sir". "Very good", I replied, "I'll send someone down to fetch them". Having put down the receiver and recovered from my mirth (amid hoots of laughter from my oppos who had heard my end of the conversation) I then changed into my role as First Term Mid. I arrive at the Main Office: "Ah, you're the fellow that's been sent down to collect the leave cards are you?" says Womble One (OOW1). "Yes Sir". He presents them to me in the fashion his position allows. "Thank you Sir": I trot off on my errand with the entrusted cards in my sticky paw. Great fun, telephones.

I hope you have again got used to December in England and that you've had a really enjoyable time in Italy. Glad to hear your new book is going great guns. Spreading out the material all over your table at Bellagio sounds really exciting, as it all at last comes into shape. (You'll be happy to know that BRNC library possesses two of your books, so . . . they aren't past redemption).

By the time you get back we should have "done" PLX/ Dartmoor (= Practical Leadership Exercise). The weather is getting really gruesome up there at present: the exception being this week's expedition when all the vicars [chaplains] went: they prayed so hard that they had really good weather. I have been spending some really COLD days on the river recently to get in training.*

* David caught a severe chill on this exercise, conducted in below-freezing weather, hauling up heavy loads. His first few days of Christmas leave had to be spent in bed.

*To H and E*                    HMS INTREPID, *Eastern Atlantic,*
                                        *22 January 1976*

At the moment we are at "Defence Watches", meaning that to get down here to 4 Deck one has to squeeze through two manhole-covers, and the Mess is completely battened down. They say it means six hours on and six hours off, but in fact it means that our six hours off this morning were six hours on as we were cleaning ship and our six hours off tomorrow morning don't occur because we are duty class. A cunning way to keep us up until 2 a.m. tonight and up again at 6 a.m. for duty.

One's first horror on coming into the Mess on Monday was that the lockers are only half the size of our kitbags. However, one can actually live in these tiny conditions. There are twenty-one of us in the Mess, with floor space of from seven square yards (when everybody's locker drawers are pulled out) to fourteen yards (when they are shut). Slightly cramped in the morning when everyone turns out. More incredible is the bathroom: six washbasins for about 60 Mids and a dozen Sub-Lieutenants. Getting up ten minutes earlier than everyone else is a good idea.

Everything is very barbarous and dirty. Your hands are always dirty through clutching at various bits of the ship, going through hatches, etc. Everything is oily from the Tank Deck vehicles. The state of the Tank Deck is amazingly slippery. Last night we had to muster there at 2200 hours for cleaning (until 2359), dressed in gym shoes: notoriously bad for holding a grip. When the ship rolled, we slid as a squad, stood at ease, six feet: in perfect formation.

At Portsmouth, when hastily unpacking, a gale warning was broadcast. Only now, three days later, has it really grown calm again. They said it was Force 8, but it only felt like Force 4. Nevertheless, all Booties [Royal Marines], Junior Seamen, and Engineer Mids immediately suffered. Last night I was standing in the passage, chatting, when an engineer rushed past at 90 m.p.h. with hand over mouth. The Junior Rates' dining hall was amazing. Every so often, all the tables and chairs started sliding across the deck. (Needless to say, the meal queues were much shorter). Eating arrangements are rather grubby. We don't have to wash up our messplates, but when they are washed up there are always little bits of grease in the bottom. An incentive not to scrape one's plate too hard at meals.

However, some of the Jolly Jacks are quite jolly. There's one Leading Regulator who looks just like that sailor with the thick neck in *Captain Pugwash** while our class PO has an amazingly long beard which makes him look like an Old Testament Prophet. Most of them like to spin yarns àbout their exploits at sea and their runs ashore. One can sympathise with the Junior and Ordinary Seamen when most of their time is spent cleaning the same old part of the ship most of the day. . . .

Things go on in their own way here. So far there has been a fair deal of time to take things easy – all the ratings work quite slowly, and it's not so rushed as at Dartmouth: just, one doesn't get much sleep. Still, what's that to us intrepid Midshipmen? DTS is the last possible "ghastly" that they can inflict on us anyway: in RN terms, the ultimate deterrent.

This letter comes to you from the Azores, courtesy of a hospital appendix case we are having to land here. Next news from Barbados in about ten days' time.

* A children's TV cartoon about incompetent pirates.


*To H and E*                              HMS INTREPID, *off St Vincent,*
                                                    *29 January 1976*


We have now reached the other side of the Atlantic in the beautiful Caribbean. At 1240 hours today we sighted Barbados on the radar and by 1310 we could see this faint, cloud-like image on the horizon. We steamed past Barbados towards St Vincent and Bequia where we are anchoring to paint the ship tomorrow before our triumphal entry into Barbados. We are going to embark four Admirals (not many ships for them these days) and so masses of cleaning has been going on. We had a delightful day today: in the afternoon, cleaning and painting the Chevrons (ship's boats) on the Flight Deck, watching the vision of Barbados and listening to our embarked band (of the Royal Army Ordnance Corps) practising beating Retreat. All with the warm sun and the beautiful rippling sea: just like the recruiting posters. It was absolutely idyllic. St Vincent, as we approached, was majestical and bathed in clouds, though also just a silhouette. One can imagine the euphoria which must have gripped the early discoverers when they came across these magnificent islands in a warm sea, so far from Europe.

Moments like that make it all seem worth while. One of the most nauseous tasks we have to do is to scrape off old floor polish from the lino with "wire wool" (= Brillo without soap) or with our knives. You scrape the lino to a light colour and then put a new coat of polish on and within a couple of hours scrape it all off again. It is so nauseating and *slow* and pointless. I have spent hours and hours in 4KI Mess (a Mess which we have had to renovate for next term's use – as well as doing the same process in our own Mess), scraping away at that wretched floor, getting ancient paint spots off. We were there 4 a.m. – 6 a.m. one day and 12 p.m. – 2 a.m. the next morning, scraping away at this blasted floor. But enough of the galley slave bit.

The temperature has been going up and up: cold water comes out hot, etc. etc. Fortunately, our Mess was an icebox before so it is really pleasant now. The engine room is now at 125 degrees F. I was down there from 0800 to 1230 a couple of days ago: fortunately, also did Rounds with the outside MEM (= stoker), so we got out of the engine room to inspect various other machines, etc. One of his jobs is to defrost the fans for the cold storage so we went and sat in the meat fridge for ten minutes to cool off.

At the moment we are attempting to recover from Defence Watches: not six hours on and six off, but a big fiddle so that we do six on and get about four off, with duty days interspersed so that when we should be sleeping we do duty. It isn't that bad, but pretty tiring nevertheless. It was Okay until we worked virtually a 25 hour day: starting the day at 0200, sleeping from 0930 to 1130, and working until 0200 the next day when they put the clocks back at 1830 to give a 25 (not 24) hour day! Needless to say, up at 0600 for a duty day, instead of 0800 as for ratings next morning. When we came off Defence Watches and I managed to get six hours' sleep I kept waking up in the middle, wondering why on earth I hadn't had to get up yet.

I must end now to whizz off to a Watch from 0001 to 0200 (what nice convenient hours they work here). Lots of picture postcards will follow, I hope: if leave isn't stopped from those bad messdeck Rounds.

Don't freeze to death in England: the weather reports we have been hearing have been abominable. Sorry I can't send any sunshine over to you.

*To H and E*                HMS INTREPID, *Bridgetown, Barbados,*
                                        *1 February 1976*

Thanks for your super letters . . . .

Here, aboard, we are all surviving and enjoying our first bit
of leave in Barbados. The RN in its typically insular way offers
car trips of three hours around the island for four people at
£5 per head (as well as going to drink in places that one could
easily find in the UK at high tourist prices: typical brainless
attitude). I have so far managed to avoid both. We took the
Barbados bus yesterday all around Christchurch: I suppose
about twenty-five miles' worth for about 25p. Choc-a-bloc full
of West Indians, all very noisy and jolly – great fun. Beautiful
countryside, with fields of sugar-cane and round the villages
coconut and grapefruit trees growing in people's back gardens.
A paradise island; I never really believed that there were
places so warm and colourful: the yellows and the greens and
red flowers – all smelling delicious.

Unfortunately, there is so much poverty. Apart from some
travellers [gypsies] with fourteen children and half a trailer, I
have never seen anything like it. Most people seem to live in
elaborate garden sheds, jacked up on breeze blocks. The
contrast between them and the department stores with con-
spicuously *white* tailor's dummies is really despicable. There
are many, many people just hanging about, with no money, or
wandering about selling things like kitchen sieves on the
streets, all eager to try to sell you *something*. Certainly not what
I had expected from Bridgetown. Somehow I had imagined
that as it used to be British, the squalor that there actually is
wouldn't be around. However, there doesn't seem to be much
racial hatred: just a general distaste for the wealthy (usually
white) man.

I found a little man on the edge of the fruit market selling
pottery: very primitive, but rather attractive for its originality
and untouristiness. Otherwise, there seems to be just the usual
tourist gear. Perhaps in the country there'll be something.

Unfortunately, there have been NO invites for Mids in
Barbados: plenty for officers and ratings but none for us (sniff,
sniff), so I don't think I shall ever see the White, Brit areas of
Barbados. What is English is really superb. The GPO building
off Trafalgar Square [with its statue of Nelson] is amazingly

like a British Residency. Also, churches are really English-colonial style. Masses of wood, like Wren church interiors, with a balcony on three sides.

I will find some postcards to enclose with this letter for visual demonstration: NB: Isn't the post quick? The letter you posted on Thursday reached me today (Sunday morning) on the other side of the world: probably quicker than in UK! I think RN post must have super-priority on RAF flights: there's certainly a lot of it. It took two Wessex helicopters (which carry 25 men each) to bring in all the mail when we anchored off Bequia. One silly thing, though: BRNC sent on my mess undress jacket from Alkit here: there's lots of room for it, isn't there?

Life aboard is still great. Good to be actually at sea, but the day is so long that when the day begins and ends it is really not noticeable. Being in a different Mess to my class means that I have to be extra switched-on, but with all the amendments and general verbal inconsistencies that go on daily orders, plus the fact that there is no set daily routine, I usually end up being somewhat switched-off. I have committed about four heinous offences so far, but only been put on defaulters once, so I've been ace lucky so far. Three times on defaulters involves thirty days' leave stoppage: not much fun.

I only wish we could get a bit more sleep. After about four hours' sleep per night, when you are listening to a stoker explaining – in their inimitable way – where all the myriad of pipes go, and what they do, it goes straight through one ear and out the other. Similarly, hearing about VHF/UMF/MF transmitter, receiver, HT/PW/TT, etc. etc. – i.e. communications – is ridiculous at 1 a.m. If you ask a question, the answer is always so involved and incomprehensible. It really is beyond me.

A rather good illustration was provided by a stoker trying to explain how, when you pushed a certain button, it made the engine valves open. He was rattling off the spiel he'd just learnt and had a diagram to demonstrate (all technical, of course). Pipe A was *in*flow, Pipe B was *out*flow. An INBALANCE (imbalance) of pressure in Pipe A (INflow) caused all these levers to work, so therefore in Pipe B, he said, you have an OUTBALANCE (OUTflow, remember?) which makes the dials register. Are your Pakistani ladies as logical as that?*

One lovely thing about shipboard life is ship's bread. When we are in harbour or up to about four days out from harbour, the stupid peasants will insist on buying ghastly cut loaf rubbish. Even when they make it in the ship they make it into sliced loaf, but for about four blissful days their bread-cutting machine broke down, so we cut ourselves huge hunks of beautiful bread.

To leave you with your hair standing on end, I narrowly escaped with my fingers today. I was attached to the catering office, and one of the ratings there told me to load some trolleys on to a hoist. The stupid idiot told me to load them on to a hoist that had not been used for four months because it was unsafe, I later learnt. When I opened the door, the machinery looked slightly cock-eyed, but testing it (by foot) it seemed to be Okay. However, when loading the third trolley the weight proved too much for it and it fell down the shaft. Fortunately, the trolley I was loading jammed it about three feet down, so my fingers remained attached to me. If the hoist hadn't jammed I would have had to collect my fingers from the bottom. I shall be more wary of thick ratings in future.

* E taught English to Asian women who knew nothing of the language.

*To H and E*                    HMS INTREPID, *6 February 1976*
                                            *At St Vincent*

Thanks very much for your letter of Monday. It sounds very cold in England at present.

I have just returned from an assault on Mont Souffriere (from the French, *souffrir*). After three weeks of gorging myself on apple crumble [on board ship?], boy, did we "souffrir". It is about 3,200 feet high, with a five mile walk to get to it. The Navy couldn't be content with just sending us to St Vincent; they had to choose an enormous dormant volcano to send its Midshipmen up in tropical heat. However, it was very beautiful coming down. It smelt like the Bucks woods in summer, when the raspberries are out. It was full of banana and coconut plantations lower down. We are now pretty well shattered, but I reckon that with a few more expeditions like that we might become fit again. At the moment, after having to wear steaming boots to climb in, my feet are dead!

St Vincent itself is very beautiful. It is very hilly and rugged and magnificent with all the trimmings of tropical foliage and native huts. The inhabitants are very friendly. All very interested to know who you are and where you are going. I think they were impressed by our madness in going to the top of Mont Souffriere. A lot of poverty, and Black Power adverts on café walls. But hostility is very rare. Best of luck with the weather!

*To H and E*                        HMS INTREPID, *Cartagena, Colombia,*
                                          *10 February 1976*

As you can see, we have had a change of schedule. British Honduras was scrubbed round because of hot political situation. However, I should think that the Guatamalans have got enough on their plate without bothering British Honduras. Poor people, [after an earthquake] it must be a disaster and a half.

We arrived in Cartagena this morning with full ceremony: twenty-one gun salute, band, and guard. It certainly looks considerably larger than Bridgetown. Unfortunately, we only get one afternoon's leave on Thursday, although we are staying from today (Tuesday) until Saturday. Still, harbour routine is good news as they don't usually get us up in the middle of the night.

We have been having terrible reports about the weather in England . . . . I do hope you are managing to keep out the cold. I expect Algy [our cat] never shifts from the towel cupboard. We would certainly be glad to swap a few bits of ice for some of the heat from out here. Last night I was down in the engine room and then doing Rounds with the outside MEM from 8 p.m. to 12 p.m. In the hottest part of the world we are likely to encounter on this cruise it was amazing down there. Every time the Chief of the Watch wiped his brow it was as if a shower of rain had fallen to the floor. I have never seen stokers perspire so much; it was literally running off their chins. Following two hours down there, with two hours going up and down four decks continuously as the outside MEM went on his Rounds, this was absolutely shattering. I really do not know how those chaps [the stokers] can stick it. On the Rounds, we took some night-time temperatures of messdecks: 88, 86 degrees, etc. It really surprised me, considering that last summer at 88 degrees I felt like doing very little: and now I was doing a full day's work at the same temperature without really caring too much. Naval training seems to make one terribly insensitive [to hardship]. They expect you to feel shattered, so that if you feel ill you don't report to sick-bay because you don't know whether you are ill or normal!

At sea, they have been getting us up most nights at 0200 hours to do coastal navigation or station keeping on an accompanying RFA (support ship). Exhaustion has its amusing side-effects. A couple of nights ago I had to stop and think in order to stop myself putting my name tally on my pyjamas when turning in.

It isn't as though they want us to experience ratings' lives. No rating would be expected to live the perpetual life of a Middy in *Intrepid*. It's just a peculiar desire to inflict the ultimate horror on us. I heard from a Chief Stoker that our embarked RAOC band were quite impressed by the experiences we were going through (unique among the Services to let its other ranks have a crack at bossing around their future officers). So, at least someone appreciates us, even if the ship's company don't.

Quite honestly, *Intrepid* isn't as much "fun" as Dartmouth. I have been trying to think out why, and I think the answer is simply being in the company of some very thick and base people. Most ratings are decent people, but some are just such peasants that they really turn me off. They won't think anything in life amusing unless it is expressed in completely base terms, and I find it slightly depressing.

On to other things. Just before we reached South America we had yet another appendix case. Fortunately, we had a Wessex on board which actually worked (the other one doesn't: it just sits there and looks pretty: shush, don't tell the Russians). Also, even a pilot to fly it, so off he went. The permanent doctor on board can only chop limbs off and sun-bathe, so of course he couldn't do anything: despite the fact that we have two operating theatres and at least a dozen medical assistants the doc doesn't know how to operate. Great stuff.

Life goes on as usual, cleaning by day and working by night: although trying to teach us tide-tables at 0200 hours wasn't the best of ideas. The high command seem so wrapped up in cleaning that on Daily Orders for the past week has appeared the immortal "0830. *Clean* into No. 8s"* (instead of *change*). They don't seem to have spotted their verbal slip. I have still managed to avoid getting three defaulters and so leave stopped. In fact I did get put down for three, but my No. 2 was so far back in FCPO Allen's book (there being no defaulters for about a week) that it remains undiscovered, and I am still on two only. I wonder if it will last me until Corpus Christi [in Texas]. In my haste to get to my last defaulters muster I went down the companion way the quick way: in one step. I'm still rather sore. Anyway, it's good to be only still on my "second". Everyone in the ship was quite excited to see if my "third" really would get me stoppage of leave, as I seem to be leading the field. Unfortunately, I must disappoint everybody – at present.

While I was awaiting trial we had a flight in the Wessex. It really was spiritually refreshing to fly into the clouds and see *Intrepid* steaming peacefully through the Caribbean. I was away from routines, and people shouting, and all the constrictions of Service life in a ship. Yeats came to mind (though inaccurately):

> A lonely impulse of delight
>    Drove me to this tumult in the clouds.
> Imbalanced all, brought all to mind
>    The years to come seemed waste of breath
> A waste of breath the years behind,
>    In balance with this life, this death.†

In a ship where Sunday simply does not exist at sea, a helicopter flight was the nearest thing.

Something I was glad to get away from was the dentist (RN-style). I had gone to see him that morning with a swelling

---

* No. 8s = Working Dress.
† Apart from the addition of "me" in the second line, this is a true rendering of lines from "An Irish Airman Foresees His Death" by W. B. Yeats, reproduced in the anthology by Lord Wavell, *Other Men's Flowers*, where David almost certainly found the quotation, at home.

in my gum and he said: "Ah, Yes. Polychronitis: let me yank out your top wisdom tooth" (tug). So he just pulled an absolutely beautiful gnasher out to relieve the pressure on the gum below, and wants to yank out my bottom wisdom tooth when we get back to GB. I reckon they are just butchers. He gave me some mouthwash, etc. to get bits of food out of the gum (which is rotting and swelling in the gum) and the swelling is going down. With luck, I will be able to cure this by diligent cleanings and so save a tooth. But really! After all Mr Screech's tender care.* And as soon as I get into the Navy they imagine they are sawing off people's legs at the Battle of Trafalgar (either that, or they think teeth grow again).

Anyway, now we are at harbour we may get a modicum of sanity back into the ship. Up till now we have been on airlock routine, with flying stations most of the time, in addition to most of the deck being painted: with the result that there are only about two doors on to the deck one can use. And obviously one can't walk on painted decks or the Flight Deck. When one is sent with buckets of this and that to do various jobs around the ship it is *maddening* the amount of time one has to take to get to one's goal. We now use vertical emergency ladders to get from A to B, and one often sees Mids appearing over the guard rails having climbed up by some obscure means.

In a ship where I have been sent to find such characters as Petty Officer Clubswinger, Leading Aircraftman Fred Freestone, and the famous PO Potts, what else but lunacy could one expect?

PS.: Please forward letter to Jonathan; I can't remember his full address.

* Our own dentist. He saw Dave on his return and assured him his wisdom teeth were perfect.

*To H and E*                    HMS INTREPID, *12 February 1976*
                                       *At Cartagena, Colombia*

I am now composing my defence for an appearance before Commander's table! Anyway, I had a really good run ashore today and came back loaded with rabbits (RN term for goodies). They have grown so prolific that I have moved 50 per cent of my kit out of my kit locker into my mattress zip-up cover, and now my locker is stuffed with native merchandise.

Life has been really marvellous these past couple of days: lots of fun. We went out sailing on Thursday, coming back with *nine* in a Dory. We started to fill up from the front, and then from the back. We put on life jackets, and I have a marvellous memory of Lieut. Ball standing up in the middle of this Dory, kicking out Mids, diving into the sea, and trying to save all his valuables, shouting "Abandon Ship, Abandon Ship". My wrist-watch withstood its water test, and we were paddling around in the sea, laughing our heads off as our ship went down (about two miles out to sea in a very large bay).

PS.: Can you imagine the deck being almost too hot to stand on in shoes? I do hope the weather cheers up in England. Our appointments have also come through. I am going to *HMS Fife*, a guided missile destroyer. Six of us altogether are going. Mark Walton and Ian Stallion you have met (both Seamen) and also three Engineer Mids. From these sunny climes (hopefully not my last run) – Love.

*To H and E*                              HMS INTREPID, *Gulf of Mexico,*
*17 February 1976*

You may be relieved to discover that even after my fourth defaulters (third, officially: one was buried too far back in the book for them to find it) I still have some leave. The myth of 30 days' leave stoppage doesn't seem to have materialised yet. Still, at the moment I am quite famous for being the King of the Defaulters. It must be my new hobby. It's quite amusing, really: when anybody is up on defaulters, whether it's for murder or for dirty language, the punishment is always two hours' extra work, 10 p.m. – 12 p.m. This is the famous Night Hawk Duty. It always starts with a crowd of half-asleep Mids sitting outside the Messdeck Cleaning Store waiting for something to happen. By the time all the gear has been collected it is at least 10.30, and after an hour's "work" the skilful Mid can start packing up; the process finishing exactly at 12 p.m. This is usually the pattern throughout the ship. They haven't really got enough jobs for all the people so ten minutes' work has to last two hours. It's really just to keep us out of our beds.

Anyway, I hope everything is going well in Mill Hill. At 0900 (Greenwich) when you are having breakfast we are just turning to for the morning Watch at 0400 (if we're unlucky enough to get it) or just going back to bed after night coastal navigation. We heard on the BBC World Service of all the ghastlies in England at present: 6 inch icicles on Eros, flu epidemic, IRA on the tubes, etc. I hope you are managing to survive all three!

Thank you for all your letters: so far they have awaited me at every port of call. They always bring a note of sanity into the world of irate Fleet Chiefs. A couple of days ago we decided that what we would really like would be a typical English Sunday. Such things don't exist in the DTS, though they may do in the Fleet. Your description of such a Sunday (even though it must have been freezing) was just the job.

We left Cartagena on Saturday and set off again on our travels, thank goodness: the heat there at 10 degrees North [of the Equator] was just too much, especially since we were fallen in on the fo'c'sle before leaving harbour for over forty minutes. It was really good to get a nice roll back on the ship again in a Force 4/5, with the spray sweeping the deck and the wind howling around. Now, the sea has calmed down again and we have seen porpoises and flying fish; as well as vultures in Cartagena.

Yesterday I went for another Wessex flight and this time actually flew it. I thought that as soon as I touched the controls the helicopter would go berserk. But in fact, with the auto-stabiliser on, it didn't fall out of the sky and went where I wanted it to go – even round in a circle. Beautiful stuff!

At this moment let me give you some details about *HMS Fife* which, if I pass the exams at the end of March (nine days after we get back from the DTS!) I will join in April. I suppose you will already have seen (being avid readers of *Navy News*) that her new Captain is (the recent) Drafty.*

She is a Guided Missile Destroyer (GMD, or DLG = Destroyer, Light Guided), D20, one of about ten which are the

---

* "Drafty" – the officer responsible for matching the requirements of all naval establishments and ships with the right personnel.

stock-pattern middle-sized ships of the Fleet and (by our standards) well armed. She carries a Wessex Mark III (Anti-Submarine) helicopter, 4·5 inch guns, Seaslug, Seacat, and Exocet, the new French anti-ship long range missile. There is a rumour that trials of Exocet, which we will be carrying out, are conducted off the south coast of France: but that sounds highly suspect to me! Seacat is of course a short range anti-aircraft self-defence missile, and Seaslug its medium range counterpart.

She carries a maximum crew of 485 (probably about 300 when we join her), is about 520 feet long, and displaces 5,400 tons (i.e. as long as *Intrepid* but only half as big). It should be a very worth-while experience, seeing one of the most powerful ships in the Fleet.

*To H and E*            HMS INTREPID, *at Vera Cruz, Mexico,*
*21 February 1976*

Thank you both for your long letters . . . . Here's another post-card to put into the collection [showing a pyramid or ziggurat from pre-Spanish times] even though there are not many Aztecs around these days. We are having a small rest at present as Fleet Chief Allen has got flu. We thought there was something wrong when he told us we could take an hour off the other day. The rabbits have now almost completely taken over my kit locker and I sleep with a 3 foot long wooden spoon alongside my sleeping bag. Most of my pusser socks have been used to wrap things up in, and my anti-flash gear is used to hold a small jar. I seem to have pretty well everything from a hat with a 2 foot brim to a frog on a bicycle made out of shells! How I'm going to get it all back to England I don't know.

*To H and E*            HMS INTREPID, *off the Rio Grande,*
*24 February 1976*

Thank you for your letter of the 17th. It sounds as if things are starting to warm up in England, now that the squirrel's come out [of hibernation] – good news. Even down here in the Gulf of Mexico the weather has cooled down considerably after the hurricane of the weekend (more of that later) and we changed back into blues today.

Tomorrow is the big day when we hit Corpus Christi: great excitement. Apparently they have been advertising *HMS Intrepid* on TV every hour: "Take home a sailor", etc. The pressmen are being flown in by the Wessex at 0645: they won't know what's hit them, poor guys. It is the first time *that* has happened, so it bodes well for the next few days. Amazingly, I haven't had any defaulters for the past ten days, so my leave is still intact. They sprang a "Rule of the Road" test on us (navigation lights, fog signals, etc.) today, threatening to stop leave for all failures. But I even managed to pass that, so, good news. After the first day when we are on duty it will be three amazing days.

The hurricane that we weathered in Vera Cruz [harbour] was quite spectacular. We were Duty on the big day, and all throughout the day they were piping "Duty Party of Midshipmen not on Watch, muster on the fo'c'sle". So out we pounded in our foulies, to haul in hawsers, put out more hawsers, fenders, etc. We snapped two hurricane hawsers (thick steel wires) and only had one spare left at the end of the day. We also ripped out a bollard from the jetty and at the height of the storm when we were trying to haul a catamaran (small, bobbing jetty) round to the stern of the ship so it wouldn't make a hole in the side, one of the outside accommodation ladders fell off: just as a Lieutenant was about to step on it. So: high drama. It really was great fun hauling on these hawsers as the wind and rain howled about us. We had about ten minutes' rest that day and were "scrambled" even in the middle of meals.

Quite exhausting, however. After three days at sea with night Conav [coastal navigation] we are all dropping off to sleep in the middle of the lessons. Today we have a twenty-two hour day from 0330 to 0130 tomorrow morning. Still, to veterans of the twenty-five hour day this is just peanuts. Nevertheless, I will certainly be glad when we get out into the Atlantic where there's only astro and evening stars.

Life on board continues in its own inimitable way. Since our arrival on board, the Mess seems to have grown slightly: but it's incredible how much kit is packed into such a small space. The Chinese laundry continues to drive Midshipmen into bankruptcy, but fortunately they hardly crush the buttons at all.

Meanwhile, at Dartmouth, as from next term, the new entry will be rankless, known only as OUTs [Officers Under Training]. How unimaginative. The heyday of the first term Mid will be no more. Other news from Dartmouth: Passing Out Parade on 12th April will be taken by Princess Margaret. You should receive specially named passes through the post in the next month or so: the Navy loves organising security!

You may also have heard the proposal that the Forces are going to receive a £6 pay rise on April 1st – a squaddy [Private] will now earn over £2,000. With a bit of luck, Middies might even be paid as much. It's pretty ridiculous really: we may be overworked, but there's no need to make us overpaid as well. When the country is supposed to be in difficulties it is typical of the government to lash out. If they gave an extra £12 per week to troops in Northern Ireland it would be perfectly justified, but to pay people grossly when they already have security and food and lodging, just so they can booze more, is incredible. For example, our pay will rise by about 33 per cent, which is totally unnecessary. If they gave us 33 per cent more sleep it would be a much better idea!


*To H and E*                          HMS INTREPID, *Corpus Christi,*
*29 February 1976*


Just a short note, due to unfavourable circumstances. The lights keep going on and off as the generators keep on breaking down. Too many jelly fish in the intakes have blown out one generator.

Today we have escorted round 17,000 people from Corpus Christi all over the ship. A solid queue from 1 p.m. to 8 p.m. when we just said "No more". From the deck, one could see it stretching into infinity.

We've had a super week (i.e. one day's leave) in Corpus. A pity we couldn't stay for another. Will write longer letter soon. Almost total blackout now, and 17,000 visitors is 16,000 too shattering. Obviously, God intends us for some kip.

*To H and E*                    HMS INTREPID, *Gulf of Mexico,*
                                               *2 March 1976*

Thank you for your letters of 22nd and 24th (Interrupted by a yell from above as an angry Fleet Chief shouts "Them that's have got Flashex [i.e. Morse reading] has better get a move on . . . and go out through 'H' section . . . and they gets two hours extra work". What a charming man: despite the fact that everybody left for Flashex about ten minutes before). It has been very nice to receive such long letters. It's great that your book *Separate and Unequal* has been launched and amazing to hear that Mark has shaved off his moustache. From your accounts, the weather should have warmed up by the time we get back. You should also have received the Solti recording of Elgar's Second Symphony.* Not much of that out here, unfortunately, though when we were around Colombia we heard the *Siegfried Idyll* coming over the BBC World Service from 5,000 miles away.

I hope I haven't conveyed too gloomy a picture of *Intrepid*. We have a lot to be thankful for. We are not at war. We are not being shot at by the IRA. And the food and air-conditioning make living conditions tolerable. Also, of course, we don't have the dreaded gym.

After St Vincent when they wanted to pull my teeth out, put me on two defaulters at once, and charge me for a kitbag I didn't lose, things seemed at rather a low ebb. They are now much better: and there's only two weeks to go, anyway.

Texas was great fun. They really do speak like they do on the films. We went to see their naval air station, where they train pilots on simulators and – trust the Americans – they climb into these dummy cockpits dressed up in their full flying gear and helmets. We then went and had a U.S. serviceman's lunch: ice cream machines, Coca-Cola machines, the lot . . . .

Corpus Christi was the supreme example of old-fashioned, 1950s and '60s middle-class America. Everybody had a big car, even if they only lived in a shack. They are all completely unworried about life, living in that "advertised", commercialistic world of enjoyable consumerland-America which I'm sure you are familiar with. Inflation hasn't yet sullied the

* Dave's birthday present to his mother.

open-hearted people that we met; but race problems and inflation seem unfortunately, only around the corner.

People are very tickled that we are here. I wore my full "English" kit: colours blazer and square, with white shirt and cricket trousers. I had my picture taken virtually whenever I stopped to speak to someone. I also wore that rig in the Junior Rates' dining hall (where we eat) one evening. A hundred faces turned my way and a profusion of "Gor Blimeys" and the like broke out. It gave Jolly Jack something to think about, anyway.

One fairly amusing thing in Corpus Christi was their Art Museum. The usual fantastic building (with dark-tinted glass to cut out the glare of the strong Texan sunlight: a good idea), containing the usual modern rubbish which they obviously think is art . . . .

Today, we have been at Action Stations (not fighting anybody though) with the ship closed down completely against chemical and nuclear attack (very little fresh air in the ventilation: the poor old stokers were sweating it out at 130 degrees F). Anyway, great fun: we were wandering around in gas masks and anti-flash gear (I had to take it away from its role of rabbit-wrapping paper)* pretending we were being attacked by aircraft. I was in the Operations Room (the centre of everything) with everybody closed up on radar and communications to all the ship.

Unfortunately, it took rather a long time before we were all secured against chemical attack, so the PWO (Principal Warfare Officer) was saying: "Eight Cuban aircraft have been reported coming to attack us . . . but they have now gone back to base to refuel". When we were ready for them, they attacked us. Jolly of them: they obviously play cricket.

One amusing story to end with. Some Mids were supposed to be chipping paint in one of the bathrooms, but were so tired they lay down on the deck with the paint chippers in their hands in the action of chipping and went to sleep. Meanwhile, the Petty Officer in charge of them came in, saw one of his mates in there and started chatting to him. Having finished chatting he went out, never noticing his sleeping Mids. Meanwhile, his mate woke up the Mids and told them what had happened!

* "Rabbits" = presents.

Like one army Corporal said to me after the Action Stations exercise today, as I was sweeping up a corridor: "Back to normal I see. Everyone busy, doing nothing".

Such is life.

*To H and E*          HMS INTREPID, *5 March 1976*

We're now back in the Atlantic and an end to Night Conav! We did however have one really super Conav a couple of days ago at 1 a.m. which made it all worthwhile – off the coast of Florida; the dazzling lights of Miami, etc. – Palm Beach, Hollywood, Cape Canaverel – all these attractive "bright lights of America" only ten miles away!

Anyway, as soon as we get to England it starts up again. Although we disembark from *Intrepid* at 0400 (!) we do Conav from 2200-0100 that morning.

However, things are starting to wind up – last night I had my last-ever Engineer Mid of the Watch. To celebrate the event they let me clean over the engine room bilges!

On a brighter side, we come into Bermuda tomorrow for a day. On today also I sent off my letter of acknowledgement to *HMS Fife*: "I have the honour to acknowledge the receipt of my appointment to Her Majesty's Ship *Fife*, etc.". I think I'll almost feel guilty living in a Wardroom after my life as a conscripted junior rating!

*To H and E*          HMS INTREPID, *at Bermuda,*
                               *6 March 1976*

Here we are at the end of our Cooks Tour and everything here is *amazingly* English (I suppose how I originally expected Barbados to be). Pillar boxes, cars, shops, churches, everything. If one took away the palm trees, the cathedral in Hamilton might be anywhere in England.

One sad note. We are taking the furniture, etc. of the "Senior Naval Officer, West Indies" back to UK as the post is made redundant. What an absolutely beautiful house he had. Anyway, like Singapore, another end to the old world: and doubtless to be replaced by something new and inferior.

So: back to scrubbing decks for the passage across the Atlantic. I received no less than *three* of your long letters today. Obviously you have been writing hard and fast over the past few days! . . . Will write at the Azores (12th) where we stop to refuel, etc. It should reach you when we get back to cosy BRNC and our five million gym periods.

*To H and E*                                    HMS INTREPID, *10 March 1976*
                                                          [*posted Plymouth*]

A last letter from *HMS Intrepid.* Our friendly neighbourhood Fleet Chief has fortunately retired to his cave in the Tank Deck and is busily planning next term's cruise: thinking up some nice ghastlies for the poor old Iranians. So while he is preoccupied doing that, we are having a very pleasant cruise. The weather is beautiful, enough sea to keep a gentle roll on the ship, and the air is still pleasantly warm without making the cold water come out warm and the air conditioning pack up.

As you have probably realised with relief I have bought a new pen (for my joining letter) [on joining *Fife*] but because of the cramped conditions of writing at present I'm afraid it will be just as illegible as ever.

The week as a whole has been very enjoyable, working an uninterrupted sea routine. On Tuesday we all played at being attacked by nuclear weapons and fallout from Atomic bomb bursts, etc. This is rather a bit of good-oh as immediately the ship comes into contact with fallout the whole ship's company go to shelter-stations: i.e. deep in the heart of the ship in the messdecks to where they hope the fallout won't penetrate. Thus, we had a good half-hour's kip.

*Later:* 4 a.m. the next morning; I never knew the implications of "Before the Morning Watch, I say . . ."* until I joined *HMS Intrepid.*

*Later:* The same day as the Action Stations Exercise we were on a day's "Supply and Secretariat Department" acquaint: "Great", we thought. However, did it mean seeing the stores,

* Psalm 130.

and systems of book-keeping, planning, etc.? Did it mean being shown how the victualling system works? Or how the Regulating (i.e. legal) side of ship's life works? No Way. Most of us were assigned to the cook's department: scrubbing out the galley and dining hall. Three of us were lucky enough to be assigned to the Wardroom: there we made up the officers' bunks and scrubbed out the Wardroom galley. Well, we gained a useful insight into the role of scrubbing out in the S & S Dept. – and that's all.

Fortunately, the Captain got to hear of it through chatting to some Mids and put an end to scrubbing out on Departmental Acquaints. Did ever such a thing happen before on *HMS Intrepid*?

We have had the usual end-of-cruise celebrations with the "Sod's Opera" (RN term for concert party routine) on Wednesday night, during which they had a series of amusing pipes; one of which was "The ship is out of bounds due to wet paint". So true. We are having Captain's messdeck Rounds again this morning, and last night you could not move in our Mess for wet paint. In a small messdeck it always occurs in the most unexpected places.

The departure from Bermuda was quite spectacular. For some reason, everybody seemed to choose the most expensive place in the Atlantic (because, I suppose, it was just like England) to get absolutely blind drunk. One Lieutenant was bounced off the pavement by his oppo, and now has a face covered in cuts. Another Lieutenant went out drinking with the ship's company and came back absolutely incapable, and another Lieut. Commander (a rather nauseating, boring, big-mouthed engineer) when trying to interfere in a ratings' argument had his face kicked in (though not with any lasting results, unfortunately). The rating who performed this service to us all is now sitting in cells feeling jolly pleased with himself.

(Later, 10 a.m.) The other day, an incredible muster took place. We were told it would be for Uniform Upkeep Allowance, which is £1 per month. When we went in we were handed £93 in cash: they had included the uniform grant. Of course, you can probably imagine the inevitable consequence: someone had his pinched. So all the messdecks were to be searched by the Regulators: which gave me rather a scare, having smuggled on board a 2 foot 6 inch *machete*. I envisaged considerable difficulty in hiding it, so I hid it in the depths of my bedding along with the 3 foot spoon, and wondered whether I would be witnessing my first court-martial very soon. Fortunately, they found a culprit before they reached us. So: another lucky escape.

(Excuse smudges on paper: hastily folded up when a Fleet Chief came in where I was supposed to be "On Watch" in the MCO (Main Communications Office). On Watch, involves being told that nobody can explain anything, or show you anything, because they are too busy. So you either write letters or go to sleep, depending on time of day.

Anyway, life goes on, as always. We were supposed to be on a Communications Acquaint today, but they haven't got anything for us to do so we just sit about flashing morse messages to each other. My own "thing" was to be the Mid looking at the Confidential Books, but when I went to see the rating in charge he said he wasn't doing them today. Then a PO comes in and says he's got a job for me: aha, yes, you've guessed it: sweeping out and mopping out the Flag Deck and under the Main Signal lamps.

You would have thought that as the Ship is SNAFU* as far as armament goes, and WAFU as far as ratings knowing their job goes, the only justifiable reason for its being *is* as a Mids' Training Ship. But they don't seem particularly interested in that side of it either. Just as Dartmouth is a rather ghastly boarding school, *Intrepid* is a rather ghastly cruise liner!

We are getting into the Azores today and on to the last leg home. From the weather forecast our track lies through six Force 8 gale warning areas: so the Training Staff may ease up a bit. One bit of good news: we disembark at Plymouth at 10.30, not 4 a.m.

* SNAFU: one version = Situation Normal, All Fouled Up.

*To H and E*                    BRNC, DARTMOUTH, *18 March 1976*

We are now back to an almost unbelievable state of sanity.
We arrived on a beautiful morning. A coach trip through
south Devon with the mist over the fields provided a perfect
"Welcome". Since then, the sun has been shining and everything is really as warm as Bermuda. All the daffodils are out,
and the birds are singing away, though everything seems
incredibly quiet with no SRE (ship's radio) or engine noises or
Fleet Chiefs or anything. The College should be quite lovely
when you come down at the end of term.

It was amazing how strange everything here seemed: the
corridors were so spacious, and life was so luxurious. No night
watches, Junior Ratings called you "Sir" instead of "You
****Middy", eating off plates, and drinking from china cups
with saucers, and having knives to eat your food with . . . .
Cooks being friendly towards you instead of swearing at you
and telling you to scrub out behind the sinks . . . . Having a
real bed to sleep in. Great Stuff. It really is a marvellous
feeling. We have cracked the first term at Dartmouth and now
we have cracked *Intrepid*. All we have left to crack is exams,
and then, back off to sea: where Senior Midshipmen don't
pretend to be Admirals.

I shall probably write, or phone again after the exams. After
Friday, when we have Captain's Rounds (typical) we shall be
able to get down to some work. The worst thing they can do
to me now is to back-term me (not throw me out), after my
amazing experience on *Intrepid*. I was rated *Third Best Midshipman* on the cruise: and not a stroke of work to show for it!

I have heard on the grape-vine that all my universities have
played ball: so long as they don't ask for interviews during
revision time I shall be quite happy.

Also, I hope you'll bring a big car down to Dartmouth at
the end of term.* There is an amazing amount of kit down
here, plus traditional Middy's steel trunk which we will be
getting on Saturday. Other news: my *machete* is now rammed
down the side of my mattress, so having survived the Regulators, and the Customs men (concealed as a pair of very long
socks), let us hope it passes Captain's Rounds as well.

* Just a flight of fancy as we only had one car, a Ford Cortina.

Love, Dave (now living a life of ease and luxury, waited on hand and foot by white-gloved stewards, etc.).

*To H and E*                    BRNC, DARTMOUTH, *6 April 1976*

I haven't written until now so as to give you the results of the exams. I managed to pass everything, and achieved a 2nd Class pass: i.e. one month's seniority. Most of us had Seconds: surprising, actually. It's just that with only nine days to revise in, after *Intrepid*, we all had the wind up and so produced an excellent set of results. I came 39th out of 80 in exams: not so staggering as my coup in *Intrepid*, but still quite satisfactory. Only one person had a First: as usual, quite an unexpected person. I proved myself a brilliant parrot-learner. Having mastered the "table" in engineering that I showed you at Christmas I came top of my class in that subject, whereas previously I had been bottom.

As usual, all the poor markers had about four hours to mark the scripts before the Pusser deadline: and then they sat on the results for five days. Typical Pusser!*

The enclosed tickets are, I guarantee, the last bits of your ticket-bound trip to Dartmouth (the Reception is after Passing Out Parade in the Senior Gunroom, with Princess Margaret). If you can remember all your pieces of paper you will "All have done very well"†. . . .

University news; in my opinion, everything has worked out splendidly. Birmingham called me up for interview, so I had a splendid day, being driven to the station, and having a free train ride (red carpet for duty travel) to Birmingham and back. Having admitted that I hadn't read anything since leaving school, and not really remembering anything about history apart from Cromwell's greatest quotation,‡ I was

---

* *Pusser*: the name bestowed on the Secretarial branch of the navy. Here it means 'the office', elsewhere it means 'in very good order'.
† The cry of the octogenarian chairman of Grace Brothers to his staff in the TV series *Are You Being Served?*
‡ "He goes furthest who knows not whither he goes". David's father had used this quotation to good effect at Cambridge and commended it to his sons as applicable to almost any question.

out-manoeuvred on about five occasions, having very little else to support my arguments than Cromwell's greatest quotation and the antics of the Barebones Parliament. Anyway, having supplemented these with the best of my RN salty stories he obviously realised that I was a harmless idiot with RN after my name: and he offered me a place.*

Reading have also offered me a place, and Durham (to my own relief) have rejected me: so that my aspirations and those of the Director of Studies will not conflict. Anyway, the next three years sound marvellous: millions of courses available during vacation, sea-going Fleet Time and the opportunity to play at soldiers in the OTC (one of my secret desires).

I shall be sorry to come out of the Navy for three years, however. My trip to Birmingham was my first time among "the British people" since coming back from *Intrepid* and I was very depressed by what I saw. The younger part of the population [i.e. students?] give the distinct impression of being wet and useless. Coming from a society where, under the most trying circumstances, there is always a joke, it struck me as depressing. I was very glad to get back to the smart efficiency of Dartmouth.

On to brighter things. I suggest you come out to Hawke . . . at 9 p.m. on Saturday evening and we can have some coffee in my cabin (can you bring two cups?), before going down to the College . . . . There are millions of rabbits I have for you, so then would be an ideal time. On the question of the sword, I haven't bothered to get one because they cost (take a deep breath) £192.†

One last piece of news is that I went on an evangelical-type

* David's account of this interview to his family was even more "hilarious" (one feels great sympathy with the lecturer who had the job of interviewing him). Apparently, his opening question was: "What historical works have you read since leaving school?" To this, Dave answered, "None". His next question was "What other books have you read this last year?" David again replied, "None". The conversation faltered. The lecturer asked about the Caribbean trip. In reply to Dave's letter about the sad conditions in Barbados, his father had commented that the slaves had been treated as chattels: and even 150 years after the abolition of slavery their descendants still lived in what were called Chattel Houses. David recounted this information to his interviewer who – realising that this was the high point of their conversation – offered him a place at Birmingham.

† His mother had offered to give Dave the sword.

freaky weekend. About fifty of us went, but I have to admit that it was too freaky for about half of us and we went out to the pub instead on the Saturday night. The weekend was full of very convinced Christians driving themselves into transcendental euphoria ("Thank you Jesus for the sunlight coming through the window", etc.). It was not really connected with Leadership Through Christianity that it was all supposed to be about.

It was good to hear that you saw round *Hampshire*.* I'm very glad that in this security-conscious Service they still allow Midshipmen's eager parents on board without five million pieces of paper!

Also good to hear that you saw *Intrepid* on TV going under Corpus Christi bridge. You were right about the very tall Mid being the one up top: he was Paul Davey; the other was Angus Ross – only about 6 feet 4 inches, whose cap later blew off and was rescued on the Flight Deck . . . . At least, one of my salty stories about showing 17,000 visitors around the ship has some basis for truth! See you Saturday.

* *Hampshire*, sister-ship to *Fife* had been moored alongside *Belfast* opposite the Tower of London. We went on board and the Officer of the Watch very kindly asked a Mid to show us all around the ship just on our own.

*To H and E*                                    HMS FIFE, *3 May 1976*
                                                    [*posted Portsmouth*]

The accommodation here is really very cushy. At the moment we are living in cabins until the dockyard have finished work on the Middies' Grot (i.e. mess). It's a very strange system. We have been transposed from the lowest of the low with all the privileges removed (*Intrepid*) to *Fife* and officers' status, with all the privileges this entails: being called at 7 a.m. with hot cups of tea, etc. I feel very suspicious of these surroundings, and would feel much more at home if they kicked us around and made us clean out the bilges.

We are in refit here until 28th May, when we sail. With a bit of dockyard delay I may be able to make the wedding, though. One of our privileges is weekend leave, so I shall arrive at Mill Hill about 8-9 p.m. on Friday.

*To H and E* HMS FIFE, *at Portsmouth*
*21 May 1976*

Thank you for a lovely weekend. It was really marvellous to get out into the country at that time of year, and very clever of you to produce such marvellous meals out of little resources.*

They have now made a decision about *Fife*'s movements. We are to go to sea next Thursday until the 14th of June at Portland, doing exercises, and then come back to have a new diesel generator fitted (a five weeks' job). It looks then as if our training officer is trying to get us re-appointed to other ships, so I think the re-dedication service will be off. I am sorry that this will mean that you will dip out on a visit to *Fife*, but if you could "stand by" to come down . . . I could arrange lunch and a tour around the ship. Unfortunately for us it means no Gib. and a re-appointment probably [means] living in the sickbay of some frigate (along with the visiting padre). But still, that's life in a blue suit.

Meanwhile, we continue to live a life of virtual paid holiday, in conditions which haven't changed much from the last century. I bought a book of old naval photographs the other day, and the uniforms (especially No. 5s, and mess dress, and tropical No. 6s – neck-chokers) are exactly the same as a hundred years ago. In fact, while having a look around *Victory* the other day I saw a "period" mess dress costume exactly the same as my own. It's incredible.

A couple of days ago we played at going to sea. I was on the bridge, being told to keep a sharp lookout for other vessels. Anyway, if we can't go to sea we might as well pretend.

* We had gone to Devon to stay with the parents of Helena, just before her marriage to our Jonathan. They pressed us to stay on, but fortunately we said we must return to see after the cat. When we arrived at our cottage there was smoke drifting from the chimney. Dave had turned up.

HMS FIFE, *2 June 1976*

*Falling Asleep in the Dog Watch*

112
A number that has simplicity
And ends in easy resolution
With which in mind
One could easily fall asleep
In peace, in quietude, and in contentment

[David wrote opposite this little poem: "Falling asleep in the Dogs one day in *Fife* I discovered that this number was coming to mind and seemed to give great peace. I suppose it was simple (11) and yet resolved, rounded up, not 111 recurring, etc. Strange, as I'm not a maths man." The night of the last, fatal bombardment by *Glamorgan* commenced on 11 and ended on 12 June.]

*To H and E*      HMS FIFE, *English Channel, 3 June 1976*
                  [*posted, Weymouth*]

Thank you for your letter with all the details of the wedding. It sounds as though it was a marvellous time. We seem to have fielded a rather depleted team . . . .*

*Fife* has now, very surprisingly, managed to get to sea and is chugging about the Oggin very merrily. In the first four or five days it was a continuous series of fires, floods and fire scares: not to mention an untold number of things packing up. But now we seem to have settled down. Fortunately, the "fires" in the missile and torpedo stowages turned out to be scares set off by the alarm system, but the Captain went suitably white and said his last prayers.

The other day we did a gunnery shoot and I went in the turret. It's surprisingly quiet in there as all the sound goes outside. All the machinery, rams, and breeches etc. is breathtakingly fast. One of the gunners there had served the guns of

* David had been prevented from coming to his brother's wedding, and very few of our relations managed to come.

*Vanguard*, the last British battleship. He said that they were really spectacular.

One of the amusing events aboard is film night in the Wardroom. The Captain is invited, and he and the Commanders (four of them: Supply, Seaman, Engineer, and Electrical) sit in the front row. The aim of the Commanders is really to entertain the Captain (and get good reports) and so when the Captain laughs, and says to one of them: "That was funny, don't you think?", they *all* go "Ha!Ha!Ha! Yes Sir".

The Captain is really incredibly ancient, although only 54. He doesn't really know what's going on, and talks about what it was like in a battleship. He represents the attitudes of the Navy of the pre-war period: as, for instance, when he actually stopped the ship during trials to give some ice-cream to the Admiral, who was passing in his yacht. He is a charming old man, but not really the dynamic, switched-on character one needs for a Guided Missile Destroyer. I am sure that next week when I start watchkeeping on the bridge we shall see him appear at the end of the Watch, waving his stick and shouting "You've all done very well".

Very few of the officers above the most junior Lieutenants know our names yet, but this can have its advantages since they never know which Midshipman has annoyed them!

I hope everything is going well and that the vegetables are growing up nicely. I will probably give you a ring when we get back to Portsmouth in two weeks' time.

*From the Prince of Wales*

HMS BRONINGTON, *16 July 1976*

This is to certify that Midshipman D. Tinker R.N. has served as an officer under training in *HMS Bronington* under my command from the 27th day of June to the 16th day of July 1976, during which period he has conducted himself entirely to my satisfaction. His pleasant, cheerful personality ensured that he mixed well with officers and ratings and thereby gained considerable experience of life in a mine-hunter. After two weeks on board his confidence has improved and with that his performance on the bridge, which was uncertain at first. He needs more determination in order to make his presence felt, but this will come with practice, and as his confidence grows – hopefully matured by his forthcoming university experience.

(Signed)      Prince of Wales.      Captain, *HMS Bronington*

# 3

## University and Christine, 1976-79

The Birmingham years were a time of contrasts when Dave often appeared elusive to us, his parents. Great changes came about: the most important being his meeting with Christine. Yet, in many ways, these just formed an interlude between school and Dartmouth, and marriage and *Glamorgan*: an interlude, not a formative phase in his development.

When David arrived, the university lodgings officer showed good sense, and probably a sense of humour, in assigning him lodgings. He had digs in Wellington Road with an old-fashioned, good-hearted landlady. His companions were also former public school boys: their short hair and sub fusc clothes a distinct contrast to the student style of that period. We visited Dave soon after term began to deliver his bike and other gear (it was easy for us as our eldest son Jonathan, then a curate in a working class area, put us up). We found Dave in fine form, and we all had an enjoyable evening together. He was vague about his studies.

It must be remembered that he had never wanted to go to university: he was there because the Navy had ordered him to go. He soon found that the regime at a provincial university was not so different from school. Courses were closely defined, with set reading lists, set essay topics, and ritual encounters with lecturers at weekly seminars. David's idea of study was to range widely over the landscape of history, stopping to burrow more deeply when his interest was engaged. This didn't fit in with the standard pattern and set him apart from most other students. Coming straight from school, and anxious to succeed, most accepted the standard pattern and were alarmed at any suggestion of deviation (it is curious that this generation of students, so anti-conformist in many features of their life-style, were desperate to conform to academic requirements).

After David's death, one of his professors wrote: "All the staff, and all the secretaries too, remember him vividly. He was always so purposeful, vigorous, cheerful and full of vitality that he made a bigger impact than any other student in his year". This was generous: but one suspects that, even more than at school, Dave responded warmly to some while showing indifference to others (who may have thought him arrogant: but this is speculation). He enjoyed chatting up the departmental secretaries: he was interested in them, they represented "real people".

Dave started to explore the country around Birmingham. On one marathon bicycle ride he went to Malvern and the Elgar country. As it became colder he wore his naval anti-flash headgear against the winds until his mother knitted him a balaclava. Not all his pleasures were solitary. He joined the bellringers at a local church, and especially he found companionship and fun in the university Officers Training Corps. This gave him the comradeship he was missing in this interlude in civilian life. One of his OTC officers wrote: "We held him in great esteem, respecting his keen sense of fun, his charm of manner, and his sense of duty. Whatever peculiar Army task he was given while with the OTC he could always be relied on to do a first class job – in his own inimitable Navy fashion". One suspects that this is a graceful way of intimating that Dave insisted upon doing everything as he had decided, no matter what the book said. He never adopted the easy way out if he considered that there was a better way of doing something.

When his first term ended, David was told by the Navy that he would spend his Christmas vacation on a mine hunter, patrolling the coasts of Northern Ireland to intercept gun-runners. This was the only Christmas when we didn't have Dave with us (or, as in 1980, we visited him, just before Christmas Day). He thoroughly enjoyed this experience, exclaiming: "This is certainly what I joined for". They didn't actually catch any gun-runners, but it was something like "the real thing".

The big event of the spring term was an Elgar concert (the composer had been the first Professor of Music at Birmingham). The programme included the evocative *Sea Pictures*, close to David's heart (he gave us the Janet Baker recording), and also *The Music Makers* in which he sang in the choir.

> We are the music makers
> And we are the dreamers of dreams . . .

What could more perfectly describe David: a dreamer of dreams indeed? Dreaming of battles long ago . . . Dreaming of soldiers and sailors who were true comrades, a band of brothers . . . Dreaming of friendship and fidelity . . . Dreaming of words and their meaning . . . Dreaming of mice and cats and larks and lambs . . . Dreaming of byways and branch lines . . . Who knows? A dreamer of dreams . . .

It was a hauntingly beautiful performance, but unhappily afterwards Dave was feeling the onset of an attack of flu and had to go to bed, leaving us to have a meal with Jonathan and Helena. Dave came back to stay with us for the Easter vac. We went down to Little Hampden, but I had to return to London for some reason and David remained at the cottage by himself. At this time he was building up a collection of miniature soldiers, which he shaped and painted himself, with enormous patience. A young friend from the big house sat beside him, admiringly.

Towards the end of the vac., Dave went off on a trip organised by his RN visiting officer to do an attachment with the Queen's Dragoon Guards in Germany. He was also able to visit the 17/21 Lancers in which one of the junior officers was a friend. So it was a good trip, and Dave returned to tell the amusing little anecdotes which were his speciality.

During the summer term we received no letters from Birmingham, though we were too occupied with our own plans to notice. I had been appointed Professor of Politics at Lancaster University and we were in process of selling our Mill Hill house and moving north. David joined us at Mill Hill on 22 July after taking part in the summer camp of the Birmingham OTC. It was at this camp that he and Christine became attached. She was at the University of Warwick, and was thinking of applying for a Territorial Army commission (Warwick did not have its own OTC: they combined with Birmingham). Christine recalls that they were instantly attracted to each other.

Of this we knew nothing. A week after Dave's return we packed up at Mill Hill to move all our belongings to our new home. The new house was smaller than the old, so we left quite a lot of more or less useless things in the cottage at Little Hampden (which we were not giving up). David remained at

Captain of the Mill Hill School Shooting Team

The Wedding Day, 8 April 1980

the cottage with Mrs Brush, the cat, while the moving-men put everything into the van. We then spent the night at the cottage and early next morning we all set off for our new home. Elisabeth and I were thrilled about the new place which was situated in the pretty little village of Hornby, in the midst of the Lune Valley, and right beside the River Wenning, which flowed, sparkling and rippling, past our garden.

David did not say much, but he evidently regretted leaving the house which had been his home since the age of four. Also, it meant severing the links with Mill Hill; the school which he cherished, and with his friends. While we were rather excitedly getting to know our new surroundings, Dave remained aloof, withdrawn. He did go for long walks over the hills and fells which surround Hornby, and we hoped that he would come to identify with the north country where our ancestors had dwelt for so many centuries. But the atmosphere was not improving: though it was taut rather than tense. At length, Dave announced that he would spend a week or so with friends in London. It must be admitted that this was greeted with relief. He actually spent most of the time at Little Hampden (he had his own key, of course). When he returned he was much more his usual cheery self. Then he went to spend a few days at Liverpool with Mark, and while there he introduced Christine to his brother. On 13 September – he had now become a Sub-Lieutenant – he went down to Dartmouth for two weeks to help in training the new entry.

At the start of the autumn term I looked in on Dave at his digs in Wellington Road, bringing some of his gear from Hornby. We did not hear from him again until a month later, when he wrote to inform us that he was buying a house in Selly Oak. Elisabeth felt that this was a sign of a growing rift between us, but actually he was much more concerned to have a place of his own where he could take Christine. Despite the move, Dave came up to Hornby for Christmas. Elisabeth was delighted; the other boys also came to us on different days and we all had a lovely time.

After the Christmas season, Dave was under orders to go up to Newcastle to join the submarine *Ocelot*. This he did; but with his usual luck found that she had arrived to pay off, and so he spent only two days at sea. Nevertheless, he reported people in Newcastle were kind, and he had a good time.

During the 1978 Easter vacation he went off to Hong Kong where he was employed on coastal patrol, mainly to stop the hundreds of Chinese attempting to enter the Colony illegally. He was somewhat frustrated because he had to spend so much of the time on board ship, often just looking across a few yards of water at the land: but he managed to acquire enough knowledge to know his way round the menu of a Chinese restaurant.

Towards the end of May we visited David in his new house. It was one of hundreds, or thousands, erected by speculative builders at the beginning of this century for a rapidly expanding work force. Teignmouth Road consisted of monotonously identical dwellings: but inside, No. 14 was unique. "Tinker Towers" was meant to be fun: and it was. The downstairs back room was the bedroom, though the bed was suspended in mid-air, balanced on two chests of drawers. The front room was for eating, with about three sideboards and a piano. Upstairs, the front room was for relaxation (though it contained a desk) and the back room was a kind of "war room" with an immense plywood spread on which all the carefully painted miniature soldiers could fight their battles. The tiny back garden contained a shed and a flagpole where, as formerly at our cottage, the Union Jack was raised each day.

We had a jolly day there; our lunch was cooked by Dave – his speciality, SpagBol. He urged us to spend a longer time with him, and next month we went for a long weekend. David had planned each part of the visit with care. On Saturday afternoon we visited Aston Hall, an Elizabethan manor house in the incongruous setting of rundown inner Birmingham. In the evening he took us to *Rosencrantz and Guildenstern are Dead* at Birmingham Rep. Next morning we visited Bournville and walked beside the canal. We had lunch with Jonathan and Helena (this was unscheduled: they now lived at Harborne where he was Bishop's Chaplain). In the afternoon we went for a long walk through – or rather *under* – the centre of the city by way of the old eighteenth century canals, which Dave got to know. It was all ghostly, deserted, mainly derelict, below the shops and office blocks of present-day Birmingham. Then we all went to a church in Moseley where Jonathan was preaching, and ended up in a Chinese restaurant, where Dave took charge. He was so considerate and kind that if we had been worried about drifting apart we knew there was nothing to bother us any more.

Helena and Jonathan had their first glimpse of Tinker Towers on this occasion. Helena noticed a photograph of Dave and a pretty girl in a party frock: she asked who it was, but was just told "Oh, that was the Dartmouth Ball". We also noticed some words scrawled in some new cement: "Dave and Chris Rule, OK", but assumed this referred to his school chum, Chris Briggs. Within a few days, light was cast on all this when Dave wrote to ask if he could bring Christine Daybell to stay with us at Hornby. Doubtless we all looked forward to the visit with a little trepidation, but Christine fitted naturally into our rather low-key family style. We went for a trip on the Flying Scotsman, as well as going for long walks in the hills. There was a quiet, easy intimacy between Dave and Christine, as though they had known each other all their lives.

Dave spent a few days with us in October, when Jonathan also came as Helena had to work in her hospital for an extended stretch. We just had trips and walks and after Jonny returned to Helena, Dave went for an all-day bike ride. The two boys seemed closer to each other than ever they had been in their school days. It was a happy time (though it rained a lot). Then, on 18 December, David phoned to tell us that he and Christine had become engaged. He spoke from her home in Lydiate: apparently her father had been astonished at the news, despite the heavy hints her mother had dropped. We were told they didn't plan to marry for a year or so. Four days later, Dave and Chris came to stay with us again: arriving somewhat late as the train they had boarded first stopped at Carlisle. We had our usual walks, and introduced Chris to some friends. She had to return to her home for Christmas, but Dave stayed on for several days before going back to Liverpool with Mark – in order to stay over in Lydiate. Christine had now left university (she had, of course started a year earlier than Dave, straight from school). She was working in a bank – supposedly to train for managership – but it wasn't what she wanted. She and David could now only meet at weekends.

David was into his last year at university. For his special subject he was making a study of a medieval monastery and its estates and tenants. This he enjoyed, but the rest of the course didn't seem to be very much to his liking. He was cryptic, as ever, about these matters. As I hadn't contributed a penny to his university education I refrained from comment.

At last there came the day when he took his degree in the Great Hall of the university. We arrived in Teignmouth Road quite early, to find Dave doing his washing. He at once asked his mother to cut his hair (which was unruly, though wavy) and then proceeded to wash that. He breezed through the degree ceremony in his cheery way. Then we went back to Harborne for tea, later going out to dinner in a small French restaurant where David entertained us with more stories. We drove back to Hampden late that night. A happy day, although Dave's academic record was less than brilliant: he disarmingly observed that he hadn't done much work.*

David's immediate reaction was that university had been a diversion, time out of his life (though he would have acknowledged that it had been an enjoyable time). Later, he was to declare that it had helped him to form his personal point of view.

With university over, while waiting for his next appointment, David spent the summer weeks exploring the country beyond Birmingham in the border counties, Worcestershire, Gloucestershire and Shropshire. He and Christine often took an excursion ticket to somewhere in the marches, putting their cycles in the guard's van, and then peddling off through the quiet country around and beyond Wenlock Edge. Here they were to discover their own personal dream land.

* As Dave observed when informing us of his result, in a postcard dated 7 July 1979.

*To H and E*                   WELLINGTON ROAD, BIRMINGHAM,
                                              *22 October 1976*

It was very nice to see you up in Brum, and thanks for a very enjoyable evening. As you can probably imagine, life is extremely pleasant up here, and every time the wind howls I think of the poor Middies at Dartmouth getting their boat tests in the freezing rain.

You may be surprised to hear that I have actually done *some* work. It did come as a great shock to me, but I shall try to ensure that I don't strain myself. While I was rooting around in the depths of the library stacks (we are usually sent to find books that haven't been written) I came across an article of yours in the *Transactions of the Royal Historical Society*, 1959. Much more interesting than what we were sent to find.

The OTC has been good value so far. The RSM is rather like Windsor Davis in the TV series *It Ain't 'Alf 'Ot Mum*. It must be very odd for him to be polite to university students, but the worst he has got out is "Listen, ladies and gentlemen. If you don't pay attention I'll have you doubling round them fields". No more of the "Get that rifle above your head and double round the ramps". But he's a great character. He gave us a lecture on the British Army the other day in the echoing drill hall: "The Paras are trained to the epitome, THE EPITOME . . ." (having found such a brilliant word with more syllables than marmalade, he trailed off: wondering, no doubt, if these university students appreciated his command of the English language). Having lost himself, he hastily concluded . . . "to what you can train a soldier".

Whenever he has made a remark to any of the ladies, he twirls his moustache furiously and looks as pleased as Punch. It is a fantastic life in the OTC. We go away for weekends, etc. But it makes me very glad I never joined the army.

Life in Brum is really excellent. It has its advantages over London in that its central area, with theatres, concert halls, cinemas, restaurants, etc. is all close together and within walking distance. Yet it is big enough to have everything that one would want . . . .

I will be coming down to Mill Hill on Friday evening and going back again on Monday . . . .

PS: I met a lady at bellringing the other night whose husband is in the Navy as a graduate entry. He was appointed to *Hermes* this year (the sister ship of *Bulwark*) which he thought was a Leander class frigate! (Now can you see why I groan at graduates).


*To H and E*                HMS BILDESTON, *25 December 1976*


Well, here we are in sunny Belfast for Christmas Day. Fortunately we've had a day's respite from chasing Paddies on the high seas to enjoy the festivities. The most junior seaman has become the Captain for the day while he (the Commanding Officer) was on the fo'c'sle heaving in ropes. For coming into Belfast, the ship was decorated with balloons and two large placards of Santa Claus hung on either side of the funnel. Our resident Royal Marines Sergeant for the duration was dressed up as Father Christmas and stood on the bridge roof holding his "reins" – leading to the jackstaff. I was, as usual (as is standard for MCMV Middies)* in the eyes [the bow] of the ship, but this time adorned with a very large red nose made out of cotton wool and red masking tape, and also a cotton wool "set" [moustache and beard]. We sang carols (lustily rather than tunefully) as we came alongside *Maidstone* [the depot ship], but we didn't even get a smile from them. Never mind, they are mostly greenies [electricians] anyway. After that, officers scrubbed out and stored ship, and then we all had dinner in the Lower For'ard Mess. After which everyone was presented with a suitable Christmas present: e.g. an enormous Petty Officer Stoker was given a tiny-weenie spanner.

Thank you very much for your Christmas parcel. It was very clever of you to find a Merchant/Royal Navy diary. The funnel markings will be useful for recognising to which line the ships belong that we board. It seems to have everything from High Water at London Bridge to dates of naval battles: a lovely present. I have also been munching the super chocolates you sent me, this afternoon. Thanks also for the book, and your Active Service New Testament.†

Prince Charles had warned the Captain of *Bildeston* about me just before I arrived, so I think he is glad we are not sweeping [for mines] and he doesn't run the risk of having his wires broken. He inquired anxiously whether I knew how to use a sextant yet.

Another Mid (their permanent one) joined us in Belfast last Tuesday, hotfoot fromn BRNC (with no leave, poor chap) so it is more fun with two of us. He is a prospective fly-boy, but when he waxes too knowledgeable I simply brush the salt from my shoulders and murmur "Sea Time, Sea Time".

* MCMV = Mine Counter-Measures Vessel.
† During both world wars soldiers (and sailors and airmen) were given small Testaments with a message from the King in front.

The weather has been very kind to us off Ulster so my stomach is OK. On the first day out, on the East coast of Scotland, it was absolutely awful with a south-east sea on our quarter. I made a mental note to take out some shares in a bucket-making firm when I got back, and on the bridge I just had time to put a fix on the chart between rushing out! I really did wonder what I had let myself in for, then.

MCMV life is absolutely great. All the officers are much less concerned with drink than in the big ships (even frigates) and it's pure seamanship all the way. None of this over-organisation and paper-run Navy, and none of those super missiles that either can't be fired because of the expense or don't want to work.

There is something of a World War II "Battle of the Atlantic" feeling doing this patrol, as the alarm bells go off and we close up at boarding stations, at all hours of the day and night. This is certainly what I joined for, and beats sitting alongside the wall at Pompey by a LONG WAY. We stop everything in sight: it seems a somewhat amateurish approach, and it is surprising that Army Intelligence isn't more forthcoming: or AT ALL forthcoming. Anyway, it is great to be earning my living once more, and I can stop being a wretched student: for a short while anyway.

I hope you have been having a jolly time with Mark and Fergie and Jonathan and Helena: and I suppose Mrs Brush is once more tucking into the seasonal treat.*

Wishing you a very, very happy Christmas and New Year. . .

* For Christmas and her birthday our cat was always given a pot of fishpaste.


*To H and E*                WELLINGTON ROAD, BIRMINGHAM,
                                 *14 January 1977*

Thank you very much for the marvellous Balaclava. It fits perfectly and is just right for this weather. I have up till now been wearing my anti-flash hood which makes me look like a Palestinian guerilla. When I go past the building site next door

I get a great shout from the workers, and old ladies grasp their umbrellas in the on-guard position.

The rest of our time in Northern Ireland was great fun, although right after I wrote to you the weather changed to Force 3/4 all the time – though that was really quite enjoyable. Boarding in that weather was great fun: trying to leap on to ship's jumping ladders when they were going up and down fifteen feet was an experience. They also let me pilot the ship into Rosyth: a very hairy experience, even though the Navigator was at my elbow seeing me through.

I am glad to hear that you are enjoying the London concert life to the full. Perhaps you would like to come up to Brum and hear us with the CBSO . . . doing a programme of nothing but Elgar: March 4th, Great Hall at 1930, if you are free then.

In spite of this life of ease at Brum I thought I might come down to Mill Hill in a fortnight's time for some quick Christmas leave. If it fits in with your programme I will arrive on 27 January in time for supper and go back on 31 January after supper and will come down to the cottage with you that weekend.

Life here is quite fun, but I miss the excitement of alarm bells going off in the middle of the night, or being on the fo'c'sle coming to anchor in a forty knot wind. Perhaps if Mrs Hollins rang alarm bells at 0300 it might compensate for what I'm missing!

BIRMINGHAM, *27 January 1977*

*Delay*

It was a slow train
We had come through under a grey plate sky
Endless estates of council houses with dogs
   in the back garden
Stechford – the industrial West Midlands
We have stopped here (The diesel is tired
And needs to be changed)
Another train moves slowly past
Heavy apathetic passengers stare out
Simulating transported cattle
The drizzle is coming down slowly

Street lamps come on, on the bridge over the line
People are walking quickly home
Five to four on a January day
It will be dusk in twenty minutes
The train will not move for an hour
It will rain all night


BIRMINGHAM, *1 February 1977*

*The Washmore Launderette at Night*
The unending chuntering of the machines is soporific
People sit around the walls on chairs
It is warm and bright like a showcase
The headlights of cars outside move up and down the
    Bristol Road
Condensation streams down the large plate-glass win-
    dows
The driers were made by "The International Dryer
    Corp, N.Y."
Just think of it – all across the breadth of America
Headlights of cars are moving up and down outside a
    soporific showcase
The world is washing out its stains at night


*To H and E*                    WELLINGTON ROAD, BIRMINGHAM,
                                        *early February 1977*

Having fun in Brum. Very nice seeing you over the weekend.
I seem to have sampled the cottage's supply of bugs. Coming
back from there I had flu and tonsillitis. Still, never mind, I
will be able to start eating again when I can swallow . . . I
shall be seeing you at Easter after all. When our big boss
[visiting officer] came up, he revealed that since there are now
only 3½ ships and thousands of Midshipmen it looks like I have
had my lot for this year. However, he did say he might be able
to get me a billet in Germany with BAOR.

[David came home for the weekend 27-31 January. We had
seats for a concert at the Festival Hall on the 28th. Dave took
us out to dinner at the National Liberal Club: as a member of

the Old Millhillians Club he had dining rights. He ordered the food and wine with aplomb. We managed to get him a seat at the concert (the English Chamber Orchestra: the main work a Handel Cantata) and it was splendid. We decided to go to a concert of contemporary British music on his last evening, with compositions by Harrison Birtwhistle, Humphrey Searle, Frank Bridge and Richard Rodney Bennett all rather avant garde for us, but we enjoyed ourselves. We had a meal before the concert, but Dave didn't eat anything. We took him to Euston to catch a late train back to Birmingham.]


*To H and E*                    WELLINGTON ROAD, BIRMINGHAM,
                                                *late February 1977*

Here are the tickets for the concert next month.* I am now back in fully working order with the aid of some super all-singing, all-dancing pills the doc gave me. I have even bought myself some new shoes, my old ones being regrettably on the point of expiry . . .

It has been a week of fun. Coming back last night I caught someone slinking over the front lawn. When I challenged him he became very obstreperous, and to questions like "What are you doing?" and "Who are you?" he replied in parrot fashion. As he refused to account for himself I wondered what would happen next: whether he would run off or have a fight. Anyway, at that moment Mrs Hollins came out, and it turned out to be the next-door neighbour who parks his car in Mrs H's garage and then goes over the front lawn to his own house. Anyway, what an obstreperous person! When I'm appointed to a submarine I shall remember to programme one of the Polaris missiles to land on his house.

I had even more fun the other night when I stumbled into Birmingham IRA HQ in a pub in the centre of the city. Wearing a combat jacket was not, I think, the best of ideas. One of the amusing things was that they had two clocks: one permanently read half-past ten, the other twenty-five past four (it was actually nine-thirty).

* The Elgar Concert on 4 March when Dave sang in the university choir, performing *The Music Makers*.

I suppose the parts inside have been requisitioned for other uses. Anyway, it's a more amusing story when it's told: I'll save it for later.


*To Christine*              BRNC, DARTMOUTH, *17 September 1977*

It's a lovely place, and it has all worked beautifully in *exactly* the same way for seventy years, but everyone deplores the system. Empires come and go, but Dartmouth never changes.

That [first] evening, when virtually no-one was there I did lots of super things that I never dared to do when I was here – walking on the carpet reserved exclusively for the Queen, slouching along with my hands in my pockets. I felt just the same pleasure as the Baader-Meinhoff gang must feel. I met the Divisional Mid (Head of House) of Blake [Division] that evening and discovered the usual brainless, out-of-a-can, very nice, considerate, polite, smart, Dartmouth product: "Do you play rugby?" Incredible.

I'm very glad I've got this ring on,* it gives super protection against anything! With my super, barnacled, illegal steaming-cap and my university haircut people didn't just shout and jump at me, apart from the Commander i/c Training who leapt at me, grabbed me by the throat, and seized my cap. Friends would come up to me and say "Dave, the Senior Sub (Head Boy) doesn't really like your cap", and my boss, (University Training Officer) would say, "Ah, yes, Mr Tinker and his cap". Awfully polite, and all jolly d.

So: I was faced with the problem: how to buy a cap with £1 in bank account. Answer: go to Gieves the Thieves, with awfully polite use-no-money system (get a shock later) . . . Having discovered this leaping blindly into debt technique, I just leapt. In one day I spent £20 on spare clothes, £30 on a sword belt and £10 on a hat. I shall have to go on the streets
. . .

Anyway, it's quite amusing to be back. After getting two plum Middy's jobs with HRH and gun-running, coming back here where they virtually wear mess undress for breakfast and clean their teeth with Brasso was quite a comedown . . . What

* Sub-Lieutenant's gold ring round the sleeve.

do I do here? I'm in charge of eleven university cadets who come here for two weeks after school before going to university . . . It's really like being a parent with a lot of children. I tell them to fold their clothes up in a particular way, take them for 6 a.m. runs, make them do exercises, solve their problems, smack their hands when they are naughty, tell them salty stories, take them on the river and tell them the best ways to skive out of things and use minimum effort . . .

I have been writing this, this morning while the GIs (Gunnery Instructors – parade staff) start drilling new entry on the parade ground below. Some were SD (Special Duties – Lower Deck men) being bawled out by their jealous instructors. Anything wrong at all is picked up. Then came some Wrens (a new concept at the college). I can see it's torture to have a new entry with no leave for the first four weeks and have Wrens about. This time, the GIs were almost polite, and didn't mention their favourite "Stomach in, chest out" . . .

I think that's about all for now. I've got a very pretty view from here and can watch the steam trains with old-fashioned GWR choccy and cream coaches going up and down the opposite bank . . . Must go now and terrorise my Middies.

*To Christine*          BRNC, DARTMOUTH, *20 September 1977*

Fortunately my boss and his oppo have gone off to RN Engineering College, Manadon, so I hope today will be one of ease and relaxation. I thought that by Monday I would have done all the work I was going to do, and would be able to escape to the Library, read the papers, and think about you all day. However, it has all been rather hectic.

My first great incident was my crash. It came as rather a surprise to me, having such a vast salty experience of being a Boats Middy, and up until the end of the afternoon everything was all tiddly and pusser. Unfortunately, returning in my cutter having picked everyone up, we weighed about two or three times as much and our momentum was much greater. Also, I was making an entrance down tide with "Springs" (i.e. fast) and as usual was making my Dave Tinker super fast approach (as recommended by HRH: so if he says it, it must be right). This altogether meant that I was going it, and when the spring tide forced me over in front of the concrete stanchion, I had no alternative but to go astern . . . There was nothing more I could do and we went wallop straight on the stem post (i.e. middle of the bows). The boat was Okay (bless her) but a large lump of concrete came out. Quite amazing. But they don't call me "Crash Tinker" for nothing.

While I have been writing this, Divisions (morning parade) have been going on, with the bands playing jolly tunes for the march past. It brings it all back – our Passing Out Parade, with all our swords flashing in the last salute to the Bridge (saluting base). Makes your heart swell . . .

These last few days have been on the go the whole time. On Sunday afternoon we had sports, and I was put in the baton-relay . . . It was from the bottom of the hill at the main gate up to the top of the hill the long way, and then round and down the short way . . . Like an idiot I said I'd go first. The hill was Okay but the pace was quite killing this second time round . . . People were strewn all over the start/finish in various attitudes of exhaustion, and it was quite a sight . . . .

Monday was a grim day (they usually are: I never go into university on Monday on principle). I spent most of the day running around arranging things . . . This magic protection from my ring seems to be wearing off slightly. "Sub-Lieutenant Tinker, why weren't you in my Divisional Officer's period? Why did you not take adequate safety precautions when bringing your cutter into Sandquay? (*into* is the right word), Why is this river list late? Not a good example, Sub-Lieutenant Tinker". . . .

I regret to say that this College has almost got me cracked. They have even forced me to get a PLASTIC cap cover (Strike me down for doing such a heinous thing) after both the Commander (T) and Lieut. Commander (UTO) have been nig-nig-nigging about it. The shame is almost unbearable. Staff officers always seem to stand between me and happiness. Just before my cutter escapade on Saturday there were a whole lot of them lined up along Sandquay watching the Bosun race. I thought "Wouldn't it be awful if I bumped, with that lot watching". Two minutes later it was all coming true.

I hope to God that I never become like one of them. They are so brainless that they all have the same type of dog, a black one, with a tail, about the size of a Labrador . . . There is only one officer who has a different dog, and he is really very human. I sometimes wonder whether they issue these dogs from stores . . . .

*To H and E*                          WELLINGTON ROAD, BIRMINGHAM,
                                                            *8 November 1977*

Things certainly seem to have been happening recently . . . The Battle Efficiency Competition went very well, with 26 teams taking part (one per company of the Territorial Army). We came first equal with B Company 5th Light Infantry. We won a shield, and all have tankards now behind the bar.* We were very pleased because there are at least four Territorial battalions of infantry in the West Midlands (1st and 2nd Mercians, 5th Light Infantry, and 5th Royal Regiment of Fusiliers). All have better kit and greater facilities, etc. and their teams remain unchanged from year to year (whereas we lose people after they have graduated). So they know the competition inside out.

When my visiting officer came up last week I asked if he could arrange an attachment with an infantry battalion for me. So I think they wonder if I know which uniform I'm wearing. The OTC has taken up quite a lot of time this term as I am now officer in charge of one of the Basic Wing sections, and with all the first seven week-ends being taken up with OTC (battle efficiency and camps) everything has been a bit hectic and there hasn't been much time for anything else.

I have decided to settle in Brum because I like it here so much. So I have bought a house in Selly Oak (with real money!). It is a nice Edwardian terraced house which includes a bathroom and heater at the back, together with the usual two up, two down, and kitchen: plus a small garden at the back. It isn't falling down very much.

I shall probably be staying there for most of the Christmas holiday . . . until I get it fitted out with furniture etc. Of course I will come to visit you in Lancaster every so often, and of course you are very welcome to stay here whenever you wish.

I must go now and do some washing.

* Presumably at the Territorial Army headquarters.

*To Christine*                                        HMS MONKTON, *Hong Kong,*
                                                          *22 March 1978*

Although I have been thinking about you an awful lot, there hasn't been any opportunity to write. The Navy is a very brotherly institution, which means one has to be pally much of the time, and because we are living on top of each other that means it's difficult to slope off on your own to write a letter . . . .

A lot has happened since I came here, and it is all new and exciting (apart from the smell of . . . dead fish and meat, garbage, joss-sticks, heat, flea-bitten dogs, etc.) . . . After the terrific rainstorm and drop in temperature we had yesterday, today it's now just like Brum . . . .

I do miss you Chris, and I wish I was with you here, but that's life. Unfortunately, my plane back isn't until 20 April, so it's really five weeks away. Everything in the East is so out of touch with the West [i.e. in the Navy] that it is just tough luck: they are so short-staffed throughout the Squadron in officers, so one can't expect them to let me go before . . . .

The London RNR has a complement list of 43 officers for their ship (the sister of this one). Here, the Captain has one Lieut with four years' experience, one Sub, fresh from courses on first sea appointment who is *Navigator* (usually . . . fourth appointment would be Navo! As mid-seniority Lieut). Apart from those two, there is ME (Lord save us all) . . . Really, we are at 50 per cent strength, which means that the Captain and first Lieut have to do six hour watches on the bridge in rotation. The Captain, however, is extremely good, and laughs at all gloom and despondency and fraught situations, which is quite incredible.

I had an amazing first couple of days. First night, arrived about 10 p.m. and stayed at shore base, *HMS Tamar*, because *Monkton* was at sea. I got there by 11.30 and was sharing a cabin with "Godsquad" Robin B. . . He comes in at 0130 and has a long theological discussion with me until 0300, by which time I was well on the way to damnation . . . Up at 0700 to get to *Monkton*, and Robin believes in leaving things to God to decide, so somehow one is never secure in the belief that everything is well-planned. Of course we get on the wrong ferry and land up at the wrong part of Lamma Island. So he says, "Let's walk": only four miles in hilly country with a heavy grip for me, and very hot and sticky. Fortunately we didn't, but the sampan that took us round charged HK$30 (£3) whereas the ferry cost us $1.

Anyway, an interesting day. We'd had a snack at 1100, consisting of chickens' feet: yes, the bits they usually throw away. How the Chinese make those tasty is amazing. Then we had a look round this village on Lamma island . . . very picturesque: junks and sampans in the harbour, houses on stilts . . . .

Time for bed . . . I love you utterly, Chris, and I miss you and long for you very much . . . .

*To Christine*                                   HMS MONKTON, *24 March 1978*

It was very lax of me not to write yesterday, but I was working – ship's correspondence – until 5 p.m. when I had to go and see my chum Chris Briggs who is an inspector here in the Marine Branch of RHKP. He's making quite a packet out here and spending it all on good living . . . It ended up with me having to take him out to dinner because he says he hasn't got any money . . . .

Today I was going through Hong Kong and thinking about you a lot . . . I can't remember where I got to in my last letter, but it was probably at the village on Lamma island. We were eventually picked up by the ship's Dory (speedboat). I had been going to bring along my raincoat to keep me dry during the passage but Robin had said "Oh no, you won't need that, they will bring along Foulies for us". Like hell they did: so we just got wet.

We eventually managed to get to the ship, which was enshrouded in fog: and we were out on patrol that evening, looking for illegal immigrants to Hong Kong. This is our role in life, in conjunction with the Marine Police. It is very sad really, because we just interrogate them and send them back, and presumably when they get back to their communes in China they are disgraced, and it can't be much fun for them. However, with four million people living in [a place] the size of Coventry – i.e. on top of one another's shoulders – that's life; and they can't afford to let anyone else in.

Navigating the ship is very different from in English waters. Here it is more like driving a bus, and you look out of the window to see where you are and to avoid shipping. Hong Kong harbour is amazing. One virtually dispenses with Rule of the Road and ploughs on. The millions of vessels somehow get out of your way.

*Saturday night*

I have lost the gist of the last page: it got very boring anyway. The reason for my not having any time to write is because of having to go on extremely boring "runs ashore". I had forgotten the crass idiocy of most people in the services in their obsession with going to a pub. It is really quite incredible. Put anybody from the services in a foreign place and they will go straight to anything English. Both Chris, my chum in the police, and Ken, my oppo on board, will not eat Chinese, go to anywhere Chinese, or do anything but eat English, drink imported booze, and go to English films: all at exorbitant prices. I have really had enough of sitting in pubs for hours on end, which is what we did this evening. I shall have to have a poke around on my own, even though I am loath to do it. Otherwise one might as well have gone to Bognor Regis.

Today I started counting the days until I can see you again. I had managed to resist the temptation last week, because it's always a fatal occupation and always makes the days go slower and last week had gone by quite fast. I was really longing to see you again today, and it's almost a month until we see each other again. I love you, I love you, I love you . . . .

*Sunday evening*

It has been very sultry and oppressive today, just making everybody go to sleep . . . We are going out on patrol tomorrow until Wednesday . . . We will probably be feeling fairly tired after patrol. Because of the shortage of officers it is a question of working four hours on watch and four hours off, right round the clock, which is quite tiring because you only get snatches of sleep and meals, etc.

We went round Hong Kong today after church with Robin, a Radio Operator, and two Chinese ladies from the Catholic hostel that he (RB) knows. It was a super tour, through the botanical gardens, markets in the streets, and streets of junk-shops . . . .

All the shops are open fronted. You hear the click of mah-jong pieces all the time from upstairs windows as you walk down the streets . . . The streets are lined with great decaying blocks of flats from the 1940s and '50s. All the Chinese hang their washing out of the windows, together with various potted plants and forests of TV aerials. The flats built in the 1970s and late '60s are OK and very clean-looking . . . The Wanchai is a particularly decaying area, immortalised in the film "The World of Susi Wong" (did you ever see it?), full of decaying bars, etc. They also have super ex-British trams here, running along the main street, following round the harbour. Only 3p for the whole length of the track, and usually packed, as with the rest of HK public transport. The Star Ferry is very cheap and efficient – 3p – all part of the super British intelligent colonial heritage.

Well, that's the end of the writing pad, so lots and lots of love.

*To Christine*                                   HMS MONKTON, *28 March 1978*

We are anchored just a mile away from the huge bulk of Communist China. Under the terms of the Treaty of Lucknow or whatever we can patrol right up to the high water mark of China's coastline, but so as not to provoke an international incident we stay a mile off. It is very impressive, this vast brooding mass of hinterland, with no visible sign of habitation: just massive hills to the waterline, giving an impression of an aloof enormity so vast that it doesn't bother inhabiting the coastline. It is made all the more fascinating by the fact that it has always been barred to the white man, apart from odd travellers and embassies. It is all enshrouded in mist, occasionally lifting to reveal the outlines of hills and coastline and the odd junk slowly making its way along the coast. But now it has closed again to a visibility of fifty metres.

Today we went down to "Long Harbour", a long bay in the north of the New Territories inhabited only by the odd floating village . . . the Commander-in-Chief's summer cottage, and some old empty houses. The ship's landing party made a raid ashore: all good stuff, no camouflage, bright blue uniforms, a ten minute dash across open sea in Geminis (speedboats) and generally a good Cowboys and Indians affair. Just as well the C-in-C wasn't at home to watch!

*Later that night*

Phew: it's getting hotter again. It's like walking round in a hot bathroom full of steam . . . Wow, I'm getting really fat here, it's disgusting . . . They have enormous meals on board, and going out on the tiles with the express purpose of eating doesn't help either.

*Later*

Well, it's now 0230 and since I was rudely interrupted we have dashed all the way from our anchorage in the north right to the south to assist two ships which had collided. When we got there (much hoo-hah on the way, important messages being flashed in, full speed through thick fog: couldn't see beyond bows) after being on the bridge all the way there, when we arrived everything has been taken in hand. Police around, no casualties, just enormous great holes in the bows of these large ships, whole compartments ripped open. Captain and Ken went to bed, Robin B. came up on the bridge, fresh, and muggins was on the bridge all the way back again. I am shagged to death, having just anchored the ship and after lots of smothering kisses to you this is going in the postbox for tomorrow morning and so to bed. We arrive at 0830, and I get up at 0700.

*To Christine*                    HMS MONKTON, *3 April 1978*

It was all go today. Returns had to be sent off, ship's books all mustered, photographers for deployment contacted, reports written, letters answered, and correspondence filed and passed around. Shitty little jobs kept landing in my lap via the telephone every minute, until the First Lieutenant and Captain went ashore, then started getting under way again when they came back. Having kept a sense of humour at it all day there is still a long letter to type to the British embassies in the Philippines and Indonesia in connection with the ship's deployment after I have left. It's just like school – with homework. Tomorrow morning myself and Ken are off to a briefing by a Hong Kong staff officer on Hong Kong (including vice!). This will take up all morning, so the Captain and First Lieut will have nobody to give jobs to. Presumably they'll store them all up until we get back . . . .

On Saturday I went round Hong Kong taking pictures. The Chinese hate being in a picture. The trouble is that they are everywhere and it is difficult to take a picture without them blocking the view. One back street market seemed an ideal place, but the blokes got very annoyed . . . It really is incredible how hard the Chinese work. They are building a new combined HQ in *Tamar* (the RN base) and you can see this building going UP day by day . . . The Chinese don't like foreigners much. If you sit next to one on a bus he will look incredibly uneasy and move away at the first opportunity . . . But I prefer going by bus and tram: more of a feeling of belonging somehow. I'm not a great believer in transporting little Europe abroad. That's why I hate American tourists, I suppose: and German tourists. Anyway, I must go back to writing this ship's letter . . . .

*To Christine*                    HMS MONKTON, *15 April 1978*

I was going to write last night, But I was quite shattered and went to bed at 6.30 p.m. and got up today at 8 a.m. so I am quite full of sleep and ready for next patrol tomorrow. Last week and this week have both been quite busy: on patrol, with only a couple of days in between . . . .

It has all been busy and good fun and has gone quite fast. On patrol it was *incredibly* busy, day and night. We practised . . . man overboard exercises and all breakdowns and pilotage.

These last are all targets set for junior officers to accomplish in RN ships, and as I am the junior officer complement I do them all! We were also sent on a mission to search for a boy missing from a sampan after it was smashed up by a hydrofoil. We also had two police launches with us and our own two speedboats out. We had our photos in all the papers . . . so it was all jolly d. Unfortunately the missing boy wasn't found, and it seemed such a waste of a life on such a pleasant sunny day.

We also did lots of anchorages, patrols at night, etc., so I was quite shagged out when I came back in – straight on to duty, of course. The Lieut. General commanding British Forces and all the Squadron Captains came on board *Monkton* that day, so it was all go, together with three ships going in and out which needed to be piped . . . I was left at 5 p.m. with a mountain of paperwork. The Captain always wants things changed. I had just typed out a letter to the new Mid who's joining, sending him joining instructions, and I had to do it about eight times before it was right. We didn't know his first name so I just addressed it to Dear Mr. . . . But his documents unfortunately came at the last minute and the C.O. told me to change it to Dear Fred, or whatever . . . The Captain hasn't been back since, so it's been OK since then. On Saturday morning I handed over my duty and had my DAY OFF.

Me and Chris Briggs and Ken went up for a look round the New Territories in Chris's car. We got up to the edge of the closed area zone to a hilltop and looked out over China. The New Territories is fun. There are a lot of Hakka women with hats and black veils with their buffalo, and Chinese with bow legs planting paddy. One of the interesting things was a square, walled village about a hundred yards long. This is a family settlement and they closed their gates to the British when they first came . . . .

Today I was the barge driver for the Captain of *Tamar* (our boss) on his Banyan (beach party). This barge is a 45 foot, two-engined horror and when I went for a practice on Friday I just could not master it and bring it alongside. Today when I turned up I was given two brand new ratings who had hardly ever seen a boat before and somehow I therefore took charge of the situation, everything went like clockwork, and my alongsides were perfect. I had been dreading today all the previous night, in my usual way. I think if I'd had a couple of old hands I would have just expected them to do things and not taken charge and everything would have been a disaster. Anyway, we all had fun, even though it poured down with rain all day, after the first sunny hour.

Normally I just let things drift on. The Captain is always saying to me on the bridge that I just stand there, dreaming, and let things happen around me, without doing anything about them. This is when he leaps around the bridge going "Starboard 30 degrees", while I stand there thinking "Well, we probably won't hit them". The funniest thing is when he puts on his aggrieved/astonished/hurt look and says "What are you trying to do to me?" The trouble is that I'm an "ish" person and he is a perfectionist. The other day when we were just off Green Island at the entrance to the Hong Kong channel we were looking out for a barge coming to rendezvous from the *port* side. Well, I was officer of the watch and looking at a rather pretty junk, all done up with flags fluttering, going down the starboard side. The Captain broke off from straining through binoculars and hanging out the bridge window by his shins and just stared in utter amazement at me – looking in the wrong direction.

Never mind: it's only four days now, and downhill all the way. I think my report from him will break the run of dazzling, superhuman-type reports I have had in the past: but am I bothered? I never have been . . . By the time this arrives I'll be back in England . . . .

*To H and E*                    TEIGNMOUTH ROAD, BIRMINGHAM,
                                              *26 June 1978*

Thank you for your card with Mrs Tabitha Twitchett: a delightful scene, with her hauling her kittens off home. I am glad you enjoyed the weekend and didn't find it too exhausting, with driving from Hornby and back. They had an article in the newspaper on Monday about the big crash on the motorway between a lorry and car which held you up.*

Even though it seems to be raining every day the reservoirs are supposed to be quite low, so if they introduce water rationing I shall stand in the garden for a shower. All the vegetables and grass are growing at an amazing speed, and the broccoli and sunflowers that you brought also look very cheery. I saw a couple of slugs on the lettuce yesterday, but there is so much of it, and it is growing so fast, that I thought they might as well eat all they could.

I am glad you were able to book seats for the *Flying Scotsman*.† It should be a very good outing, even though once in the carriages it won't be much different from normal, apart from puffs of smoke going past the windows. It is usually quite amusing to see photographs of these special trains with a long line of heads jammed out of every possible opening.

Would it be possible to stay at Hornby for a few days over that period and bring Christine Daybell along too? The rough dates I had in mind were July 24-27, if that is convenient for you. With luck, that should be the hot season!

For the next couple of weeks I shall be at camp and then hosting Chris Briggs and his enormous appetite (he has expanded to his former self again after his enforced army slimming). We'll be going around England in his ancient car. However, I haven't heard from him yet . . . .

* We arrived at Dave's house about an hour late as traffic was brought to a complete halt on the M6.
† This was a special trip organised for steam-train buffs from Carnforth around the coastal line which goes over bays and promontories to Ravenglass. [We had a lovely trip, with dozens of holiday-makers waving at our train: "Just like being the Queen Mum", as I observed to Dave.]

*To Christine*                    TEIGNMOUGH ROAD, BIRMINGHAM,
                                              *2 September 1978*

I looked up St Helens in the AA touring Guide today, and it actually had an entry so it can't be that bad* . . . Did you know Sir Thomas Beecham was born there? Who's Sir Thomas B you ask?

Did you know that, when Canute, that ruler of the Nordic Empire of England, Denmark and Scandinavia went to hear the monks of Ely Cathedral sing evensong he was moved to

* Christine was to start working in a bank at St Helens.

tears? Not altogether surprising when you consider that vast, flat landscape with the odd small village here and there and without any real towns. All solid men, toiling at their farm-work – five days' work on their lord's land, one day of rest on Sunday, and one day left in the week to cultivate their own ground. Then you come across a tall, vast cathedral (just newly built then).* So, if you are a king collecting Danegeld and revenue from your vast kingdom, how petty compared to these rather illiterate Saxon, and later Norman landholders, whose whole experience is based on ploughing and work, horses and rents, yet they are contributing with a will to raise a building and its pillars higher than ever before in a sublime architectural conjecture of beauty. Most of them will never see its completion, but will leave it to their descendants. How completely incongruous with a society that buys and sells churches as convenient units of rent. No wonder Canute was moved to tears . . . .

Tomorrow, 3rd September, is the anniversary of the death (and of his two greatest battles) of Oliver Cromwell, that ace-hero of all good Protestants who bashed every Wop, Paddy, Scot, Royalist, etc. in sight. If you examine the thoughts and ideas of those ten glorious years of the English Republic they are so far in advance of their time that it's not true. Here was the "Norman Yoke" at last cast down (or nearly).

Going on to 8th September, when our first year is up, I hope you realise that it is the Feast of the Nativity of the Virgin: who some Pope said didn't count any more, just like poor old St. George. It also marked the end of summer in the medieval agrarian calendar, and all the peasants heaved a sigh of relief as they didn't have to do boon work any more: work which was supposed to be out of favour to help their lord, from which he granted them stacks of food because he was so happy. But, such is life, this became compulsory as long as he gave them a bit of old cheese.

If you have some spare time between rushing from one place to another I shall take you out to dinner to celebrate (because living on bread and macaroni cheese is quite cheap). If you have recovered from all your travels by then we could go to

* After the first building was destroyed by the Danes in 870.

Gloucester or Lichfield to relax and explore the cathedral and the tea shops.

*To H and E*        Teignmouth Road, Birmingham,
*4 April 1979*

Thank you very much for sending me a cheese-board. I can never remember when my birthday is so I was very surprised when it turned up. I hope your students aren't writing more essays than you can cope with and that the garden is getting on well. Everything here took quite a battering from the winter as we had ice on the ground from mid-December until mid-March, so it had cracked up everything underneath. I think it was the only place in England where the snow hadn't melted by March. The birds were all very pleased with your bird-bag of peanuts and I think we had all the bird population of Selly Oak here.

Hope to come and see you at Hornby at Easter.

# 4

## *Hermes, the Cottage, Glamorgan, 1979-1982*

In the autumn of 1979, David and Christine were looking ahead to their wedding in six months' time. They thought about getting a home and they decided that they could either afford a small, modern "box" or else a rather run-down cottage. They searched around their favourite county, Shropshire, and came across a tiny old cottage at Clungunford. The asking-price was excessive for what Dave always affectionately referred to as "his ruin". They made an offer. It wasn't accepted. Instructions for his next appointment did not reach him for a bit because they weren't in Selly Oak. When he caught up with the Navy's letter it directed him to join *HMS Hermes*, the largest ship in the Fleet. In order to join he had to fly the Atlantic as the carrier had arrived at the vast American naval base in Norfolk, Virginia for a NATO exercise. Dave saw little of the Old Dominion. *Hermes* has the reputation of being a happy ship, but Dave was not altogether happy in his return to the Navy. The years at Birmingham had unsettled him, while he regarded the enforced separation from Christine as a hole in his life.

Christine had discovered that a career in a bank was not for her, and so she decided to become a regular officer in the Women's Royal Army Corps. This would enable her to play more tennis and to compete in championships. So off she went to the WRAC Officers Training School. Meanwhile, the cottage at Clungunford was offered to them at a price they felt was less unreasonable. They decided to buy, and Christine handled the purchase with David on the other side of the Atlantic.

Soon after David's return we were able to see him again when he came to visit for Christmas. He rather surprised us by announcing that he was transferring from the Seaman branch of the Navy to the Supply branch. The main reason he gave was that he would be more likely to serve in a shore establishment and so share more of his life with Christine. But, though he did not tell us, his decision was related to a growing doubt about the "system". He was not ambitious to command, and he regarded the exercise of command as often arbitrary, without reason. His friends had tried to dissuade him, but as always he made up his own mind.

The result was that he had to embark upon more courses to qualify for his new specialisation. First, he returned to Portsmouth to the great navy complex which goes under the name of *HMS Nelson*. He endured his renewed exposure to training with increasing cynicism.

However, the great event of this Spring of 1980 was his marriage to Christine. The wedding was held at the Catholic church of Our Lady at Lydiate. Although this former village has now become a commuter suburb of Liverpool the church stands on the edge of green fields, and has a rural atmosphere. Dave and Christine devoted considerable care to the form of the service. The Roman Catholic Canon (a friend of Christine's family) who conducted the service graciously asked Jonathan to deliver a sermon, which he did felicitously. The ambience was provided by friends in the Services – a mixed guard of honour, naval and military, formed the archway of swords under which they emerged. Daffodils waved in the grounds of the church and created a background of freshness and verdant delight to the inevitable session with the professional photographer which followed. Then they stepped into a white, open Rolls Royce and headed for the reception. Passing a Corporation refuse truck the Bin Men gave them a cheer, and they cheered back.

At the reception, David handed me a key to their cottage, asking us to go there whenever we wanted. We did call in at Clungunford one weekend and were delighted to find Dave and Christine there, somewhat grubby, working away at the restoration of their cottage. Typically, Dave insisted on ripping out all the accretions and starting again with the bare walls. It was a bold (and to me, somewhat frightening) decision; justified in the end when the old cottage began to reappear in its ancient simplicity.

After the wedding, David moved to Chatham to take yet another course at the Supply School. When we asked him what his job would be, he retorted "Dishing out the Mars Bars". When I pointed out that the Supply Branch also provided Captain's (and Admiral's) Secretaries, he observed that these appointments only went to those who were very keen (implying that he wasn't). However, when the course was ending, it transpired that he was to be the Secretary of the Captain of *HMS Glamorgan*, a sister-ship to *Fife*. Dave neither exulted nor complained; though he knew that this meant that his hopes of having more time with Christine must now be given up.

Because as Captain's Secretary he would have to handle confidential and personal papers David was given an extra tough security clearance. We swapped reminiscences: I also had to be checked before doing a job for the Foreign Office. I told Dave that my man had asked if I had ever belonged to CND: I hadn't, but I gave a so-what answer. Dave then revealed that he had told his man that if ever he was appointed to a Polaris submarine he would refuse to serve. His inquisitor recorded this without blinking. Perhaps, rightly, he deduced that this implied no lack of patriotism.

The time in *Glamorgan* is fully described in the letters. After his death, a senior officer recorded: "He had made a great success of his job on board. The relationship between the Captain and his Secretary demands a particular skill, and David had developed this most ably .... He was quite unflappable and preserved an efficient air of calm when matters were at their busiest. He led his staff, both in the Ship's Office and on the Flight Deck admirably and always achieved the best from them." As the letters reveal, the outward display of efficiency was achieved at the expense of some inward tension.

It was quite usual for the Captain's Secretary to double as Flight Deck Officer, controlling the departures and arrivals of the ship's helicopter. During their normal regime of time in port, exercises, and trials, this part of his duties was only incidental to the demanding and multifarious tasks of Captain's Secretary. In addition, David carried out other routine duties laid upon junior officers.

So time passed; counted by David mainly by the days and weekends he was able to spend at Clungunford. Christine was with the Artillery at Larkhill, and they contrived to get to their cottage whenever the opportunity opened up. Then Christine was posted to the Royal Engineers at Chatham. Time together, and time at the cottage, was not so easy to obtain. But he was getting towards the end of the normal duration of his appointment on *Glamorgan*. A move to Chatham would be ideal, but the Chatham base had been scheduled for closure by the Government. It didn't seem likely . . . .

Captain Barrow, in command of *Glamorgan*, was active on behalf of David, who learned in September 1981 that he *would* go to Chatham as Secretary to the Chief of Staff to Flag Officer, Medway. The future looked good. Meanwhile, *Glamorgan* was to proceed to the Persian Gulf to represent the Royal Navy in that troubled area. The story of what happened to the ship, and why they came back prematurely is fully told in the letters. The necessary repairs were rapidly completed in Portsmouth Dockyard and the ship returned to sea – to the routine of fleet exercises, of which Dave felt he had already experienced enough. Late in March 1982 they set off for Gibraltar for a big NATO exercise, *Springtrain*. David made the best of yet another parting from Christine by telling himself that this was his last time away from her.

*To Christine*         RAF BRIZE NORTON, *1 September 1979*

A hectic day yesterday rushing around, with Ken [a university friend] doing all the dirty jobs, washing up, getting my shoes, etc. What a good man to have in the house! The kitchen looked absolutely spotless when he'd finished. He's being very kind, coming in every day to show people round the house.

Lots of exciting news about the cottage, and selling the house, which I should have phoned you about. Poor you: no rest at all for the next two weeks . . . with solicitors and surveyors.

Last night was very enjoyable coming down to Brize Norton. I don't think I will ever travel 2nd Class again. In the 1st you have a whole compartment to yourself and a feeling of utter snobbery. The guard never asked for my ticket or even gave me a second look. When we were at Swindon waiting for our bus to Brize Norton there were about four people waiting, until five minutes before the bus went when about a hundred drunken sailors lurched out of every conceivable pub, singing songs and joking. These blokes, who come from a background of yobbery, develop such a sense of humour and discipline. Even though they were all "gone" they were still in control of themselves and knew how far to go in ribald jokes. They were very amusing on the bus back . . . .

*To Christine*                    HMS HERMES, *3 September 1979*
                                          *Norfolk, Virginia*

I love you so much that I miss you incredibly. However, it is not very long until we see each other again, and then we will be very happy. This is just a private minute or two in a very public life, and when I think of you it's hard to keep back the tears . . . . Writing to you, Chris, is like reaching out to touch you. I wish I could prolong it for ever.

*Hermes* is a very good ship, with plenty of friendly and amenable pussers and chaplains and junior officers. But it's a bit difficult to get used to this very open life. I drink every evening, late. Trying to find something to say is very difficult. After you have talked to a good friend for a long time you just run out of things to say.

"Hurricane David" is moving our way from the Caribbean, so we will probably zap off to sea for a couple of days to avoid it.

*To Christine*                    HMS HERMES, *4 September 1979*

The last letter was written in rather a homesick way, as it's such a strain when we are separated, forcibly, and especially after we'd had such a lovely two months together . . . . However, it has started to wear off now, especially after I've realised that there are four of us here who feel exactly the same . . . . It's really a question of leading our separate lives enjoyably and seeing each other for a week-end every month or so. There is absolutely nothing I can do about it. I can't fail my Fleet Board, because they have got wise, and don't fail graduates, and I can't resign for five years. However, though we lose on the swings we gain on the roundabouts . . . you'll be able to follow a career, and when we see each other we will enjoy every moment of each other's company, whereas people who have a normal marriage have to . . . save their loot to pay for a never-ending mortgage and see each other every night, appreciating each other less and less, sat in front of the telly. At least we'll be looking forward to our time together, and as you are in the Army you won't be weighed down with domestic worries and responsibilities with no one to help you, which is the thing that wrecks a lot of naval marriages. With friends around you (even though they'll all be men!) it should give you any security you need.

Enough patronising philosophy: better things follow in the next letter.


*To H and E*                          HMS HERMES, *4 September 1979*

As you so rarely get letters from me you won't be surprised to learn that this is a begging letter: more of that later.

I phoned at the end of last month, but I think that by then you had gone to Italy. . . . I joined *Hermes* eventually on 1 September. Quite a feat, without being court-martialled at the end of it (the Commander's wrath and punishment is still to come). Christine and I had a wonderful month together, visited about twenty-six stately homes and ate about twenty-eight Chinese dinners.

"Hurricane David" which has swept through the Caribbean is making us leave Norfolk, Virginia tomorrow, and we will stay out at sea until it is over and then come back and pick up the pieces. There are literally a dozen enormous aircraft carriers at Norfolk (the *Nimitz* and the *Eisenhower* each hold 6,000 men) and *Hermes* is dwarfed in comparison. It really is the last years of these great ships and in twenty years' time this sight just won't be able to be seen.

Living on board with no privacy at all, sharing a grot with other subs, and having people around you every minute of the day – even in the toilets – was quite strange at first. But my old life-style in *Fife* is all gradually coming back. Quite a change from university life.

It is also strange being with all my old friends from three years ago. Everybody has been away for three years, and we are just as green and inexperienced again. Quite a lot of my old chums have also got engaged, and have either left the Navy or are wondering whether they can face five years of separation: so the Navy really has goofed by sending us to university.

The begging part of this letter is about the cottage in Shropshire. After the deal fell through once, it revived itself again, and the price finally reached was £13,000. We have decided to sell Teignmouth Road, which should go for about £9,000 or maybe more, and we have arranged with the bank for bridging loans and improvement loans to £9,000 and we wondered if you could give us a loan of £5,000 which we would start repaying as soon as we had repaid the bank (about the middle of next year) . . . .

Christine is dealing with everything . . . so I would be grateful if you would write to her via Teignmouth Road . . . .

I'm sorry that the first letter I have written to you for about two years is asking you for cash, but that's pretty typical of me.

Anyway, hope to see you at Christmas.

*To Christine*                    HMS HERMES, *5 September 1979*

This is a jolly good prison, you know. We work from eight to twelve and then it's all free. However, Norfolk is twenty miles away and it's two miles to the Dockyard gate. I haven't actually been anywhere, because there weren't any trips left and you can't otherwise get out without a car. I'm not particularly bothered. I always get very mean when I'm on board and really begrudge spending £5. In both ports the ship's company has spent a total of £1,000 per head. The Cash Pusser gets $1½ million twice a week from the bank (only taking two Midshipmen and three briefcases in a Land Rover). When the ship sails, we are going to be anchoring about a mile from Scotland after four days' sailing. But we are not going to come into harbour until 10 October. This is so we each get an extra £60 local overseas allowance. You receive it at the rate for the last port of call until you touch England. Ridiculous: they're a mercenary lot here!

I think *Hermes* is the best ship I could have joined. None of this standing on the bridge all day, and then a night watch, and then typing out the Captain's odd jobs as in *Monkton*. There are stacks of nice pussers, a couple of nice padres, two of my best old chums, and everybody is very friendly and helpful. Of course there are aloof $2\frac{1}{2}$ ringers (Lieut. Commanders) who don't talk to Subs . . . but in a big ship with 1,300 men and 150 officers it just doesn't matter. The RC chaplain is always a real laugh, and we have some good times. I like drinking in the bar with these people. I can just relax in very pleasant company. My old bosom pal from *Intrepid*, Gaius Hiscox is also here. He has been through the same things vis-a-vis University, the Navy, getting engaged, leaving, etc. A lot of people who I liked at Dartmouth have left because of these reasons. Also, Graham Owen is here: a great friend from University, going through exactly the same things (he's a pusser). Another pusser is Mike Shreve, I hadn't met him before: also thinking exactly the same things, also marrying a Catholic on April 7th . . . .

*To Christine*                                    HMS HERMES, *7 September 1979*

Some good news on the ship's movements. We'll be getting to Portsmouth on 10 October . . . . I have so far escaped the Commander's wrath, because it was so long ago [that joining instructions were sent] he didn't put two and two together when he interviewed me. I was really scared that he would remember when he was asking me questions about where I had come from.

Yesterday I was duty [officer] (we do gangway watches) for a day, when Admirals were coming and going, with an official cocktail party in the evening. I was in and out of about ten different rigs and wore my smartest uniforms: tropicals look really smart, and I'm sure it would have made you go all of a flutter.

I'm glad you went to Clungunford again – I wish I could

have gone with you. I hope you took the keys and had a good look inside . . . .


*To Christine*                    HMS HERMES, *8 September 1979*

Had another lovely letter from you today . . . . You have been having a busy time all round. Sounds just like gangway duties here: problems arise, one after the other, during the day, and they just have to be sorted out. When the Duty Lieut. Commander and the Officer of the Day are around they cluck like mother hens, saying "Have you done this? Have you done that?" This morning I was up there with a series of responsible ratings who knew exactly when they had to turn up for various duties and were very competent: and these officers were panicking, getting me to drag up these ratings about fifteen minutes before they were required. The First Lieutenant had booked transport for 12.30 and the duty driver knew to come at that time. At 1225 the First Lieut. came up panicking, saying "Where's my driver? Why isn't he here? I'm going to miss my match! Ring him up, get him here; you should have rung him up ten minutes ago." He took about three minutes to have a really good panic: the bosun's mate was on the phone dialling the driver's mess, the First Lieut. was tearing his hair out – when the duty driver just turned up, perfectly on time as arranged.

I always enjoy gangway duty because it is a very good exercise in not panicking and sorting everything out. The key is not to fluster when senior officers leap on your back in a state of high agitation: write everything down, and deal with things when a big panic is over and a lull is on. This is my second duty in three days, and it's been very enjoyable, but I have got a good Quartermaster and Bosun's Mate who I can rely on.

Somehow duties and things seem to have got in the way of going ashore, but as I am such a Shylock on board I'm not bothered. I haven't spent a single dollar since I've been here . . . .

I really wish we were getting married in December, and didn't have to wait until April. It would be worth eloping for:

I'm sure the RC Chaplain on board would be only too happy
to oblige . . . .

*To Christine*                          HMS HERMES, *15 September 1979*

Life in the grot is pretty good on the whole. Mike Shreve
makes it worthwhile, and swings the balance as he is very
intelligent and interesting to listen to . . . . All the other chaps
are very pleasant.

Today has been a bit grim in the grot because Punk Rock
has been blaring away all day at a million decibels and the
telly has been fixed so that's been blaring away as well (the
ship pushes out its own music and telly). There hasn't been
any time to relax and enjoy some quiet but tonight I borrowed
Gaius's cabin while he was helping to show the Wardroom
film . . . . When there's non-stop loud music, and people
shouting over the top of it to make themselves heard, you just
can't think. Anyway, it's only a minor hassle in a ship which
is very good.

*To Christine*                          HMS HERMES, *20 September 1979*

Tomorrow is halfway through the cruise, and on Sunday
I'll get two weeks' worth of letters from you – lovely! . . .

Crossing the Atlantic has been very smooth. We've got
about a ten foot swell on now, but even in the stern where the
grot is the movement is quite pleasant. The most amazing
thing is the vibration. Jim Palmer made a tape of people
talking and you can't hear the talking for the noise of shaking:
just like an earthquake. In our pits [bunks] at night we always
get rattled around a bit, but it's usually just amusing. It's
these silly Seamen winding the ship up to 20 knots and then
stopping, or only using one shaft, etc. Stupid games they
play! . . . Meanwhile, Commander S (Supply) has been pe-
rusing a biography of Clausewitz in his cabin as the stewards
bring him regular cups of coffee and biscuits while the Atlantic
gently swooshes by on the outside of his stateroom bulkhead.

Ah, this is the life! Once you give the Seamen silly games to play, to keep them happy, life becomes civilised. However, they've finished their games this weekend, so we've been having bollockings: for no reason: just that they aren't occupied.

We had an interesting talk with Commander S about where our appointments are likely to be. One of my first three jobs will be ashore, and then I will be Supply Officer of a frigate . . . . The higher up you get, the better the jobs become, and it is very tempting to stay in for a career. At about thirty, if I haven't been courtmartialled or deserted by then, it might be very tempting to stay in. I can't decide which is the lesser of two evils: working in a frigate, being sick and cold and wet when we have to act as Flight Deck Officer, or being in a nuclear submarine, being at Faslane, and standing periscope watches . . . . But that's life.

*To Christine*                    HMS HERMES, *22 September 1979*

It is difficult to write very personal letters in the grot as there's always music/TV/people coming in and out, and somehow the really deep feelings I have for you just don't surface, so these letters just contain everyday things . . . .

We are not very far from you — about 45 miles off Northern Ireland – but by the time you receive this we will be up towards Iceland, protecting the northern gap through which the Russians will come. We have already been overflown by two *Bear* Russian reconnaissance aircraft and *Kresta II* with its A.G.I. – intelligence-gatherer trawler – has been shadowing the group (*Kresta* is a cruiser with stacks of missiles and torpedoes, their latest and biggest). I am doing bridge watches for the first week of the exercise, so that will be interesting, if slightly stormy. But the real action happens in the Operations Room (there are two on board) where all the Seamen shout at each other even more, and put plastic ships on top of radar blips on big plotting tables and move them about and get terribly excited . . . . At the moment, excitement is mounting at the prospect of mail. Ninety sacks are waiting for the *Hermes* at Oban, and lots from you . . . . The scrabble for letters in the Wardroom is supposed to be phenomenal: 190 officers just scrummaging for anything that's got their name on it. The mail never gets to the pigeon holes . . . .

*To H and E*                    HMS HERMES, *23 September 1979*

It has been very nice of you to write so many letters and post-cards to me while I have been in *Hermes*. I was really horrified to hear what was happening to Mark . . . . I hope you have been able to give him the peace and support that has been taken away from him and I'm glad he is staying with you at Hornby.

I will write to the solicitors and get them to put the loan on a legal basis . . . . Anyway, to talk about more pleasant things, life is very pleasant on board *Hermes*. I shall be doing bridge watches next week when we start *Exercise Ocean Safari*, so it should be very exciting. It promises to be quite rough, as we are protecting the Iceland-Scotland gap, looking for enemy submarines with our helicopters. It is a very smug feeling to look out seeing frigates ploughing up and down through the waves while *Hermes* moves about three inches! If you would like to come down and have dinner on board while we are in Portsmouth I would be very pleased to entertain you and show you round *Hermes* . . . . While we are on exercise we don't, of course, get any mail so we have been looking forward to this mail drop today for two weeks. Everybody is very jealous of me cos I had twenty letters altogether! The last letter I had from Christine was on Monday 17th, when she had just got to Camberley . . . I'm sure she'll get on fine . . . . I have had a letter from her saying that the cottage is full of wood-worm: just like Tinker Towers! I hope she can manage to take you down to look at it sometime as it really is a dream cottage. And of course, any time that you would like to spend a short holiday or weekend there, just write to us and we can give you the keys. It is at the foot of the Welsh mountains and in mixed arable and cattle country – very lovely, though it is hilly for cycling. I hope we can all go to see it sometime, maybe at Christmas . . . . Hope to see you at Christmas.

*To Christine*                    HMS HERMES, *28 September 1979*

This week has really flown by . . . . We are now ending the period of limited war which began on Thursday . . . . Yesterday morning I was on watch when the war began: very unimpressive. We were promised a large air attack from the air force bases in Scotland, and I had visions of a hundred aircraft strafing the Fleet. But instead, all we had was two Phantoms/Buccaneers every half hour flying overhead dropping a thunder-flash on the *USS Dale*'s splash target . . . . We usually also have a couple of Russian *Bear* reconnaissance aircraft overhead. The Captain was a bit annoyed today and trained the Seacat missile launchers at them . . . . The only other Russian we've seen has been a *Krivak* missile-armed destroyer hovering around, but she left two days ago. Things have been warming up on the bridge and this afternoon we had a submarine wolfpack attack on us . . . . When it's nice and peaceful up there I think it's very nice being on the bridge, just ploughing through the waves with a 20,000 ton aircraft carrier beneath you. But that's not a Seaman officer's life. It's more continual panic stations . . . .

The other day we had an emergency landing on deck, and just as we were coming to our course into wind, for receiving the helicopter, the quartermaster on the wheel steered the wrong way. The officer of the watch started giving quick wheel orders when the Captain yelled down the intercom "You're panicking bridge: stop panicking", and then strode on to the bridge, thumped the officer of the watch, and proceeded to do a Corporal Jones act [from *Dad's Army*] shouting "Don't panic" . . . What a performance. Things would have sorted themselves out quite happily if all this shouting hadn't been going on. I felt quite shaken up about it . . . the sudden danger of the helicopter crew possibly losing their lives, the shouting of the Captain, and things going wrong at critical moments . . . .

However, bridge watchkeeping does have its lighter side. I am always utterly at a loss up there. One of my jobs is to answer telephones. People ring up with utterly incomprehensible messages, like "The 660 is on jacks". I never know whether they require an answer, or action, or anything.

The Navigator also gives me a few silent laughs . . . . He's always fuffing around the chart table, drawing in strange lines and making weird calculations. He'd just finished, and said to me "Where's the 10 o'clock fix?" When I said that I hadn't put it on he replied in a voice of utter horror "But it's 1002". They do tend to get worked up, whether we are following these little lines or not: miles from anywhere.

*To Christine*                    HMS HERMES, *28 September 1979*

This is the end of my notepaper: eighty sheets since I left England, and most of it to you. Fortunately we haven't had a gale today so the mail is going off as planned. Replenishing is really hairy in heavy seas. Today it was about Force 4-5 when we were replenishing. Two ships, steaming together about 120 feet from each other, and both rolling. The effect on the jackstay and the goods being transferred on it is quite dangerous: the load leaps from about 10 feet above the sea to 60 feet above in two seconds, and back again. The blokes unhooking the loads from the jackstay have a dangerous job: it's surprising they don't lose their hands and get crushed by a load which suddenly jerks off the deck and crashes down into it . . . .

Fortunately, these storms we have been having (we have been up almost to Iceland and are now off the coast of Norway inside the Arctic Circle) aren't affecting us because the RN has these really good pills – guaranteed 200 per cent success . . . . They were originally developed to combat diseases of the middle ear, which is all to do with your stability, etc. . . . .

One of our recruiting officers has played a huge joke on us. We have on the bridge a radio operator who relays messages around the ships in the Fleet, and so therefore is pretty vital. One is a completely unintelligible Scotsman, and my job is to take messages from him. He will say: "Wuchel mackgruckel twulv brechel proluchs", and no matter how many times I ask him to repeat it I never can understand him. It has been suggested he ought to have a blackboard . . . . Fortunately, the officer of the watch who does bridge-keeping regularly can grasp the odd word . . . .

*To Christine*                          HMS HERMES, *2 October 1979*

We are now working with the Air Engineering Department: an extremely pleasant bunch . . . . I had really had enough of being on the bridge, getting shouted at, by the end of the week . . . . The war became more and more intense each day until it finished on Saturday . . . . On the bridge the Captain has an intercom system to many parts of the ship. One time . . . the Captain, very irritated, picked up the phone and said in a cross voice "I don't know what's going on, but THIS is the CAPTAIN". A short pause: "Well, this is the Admiral".

During one of the watches we were steaming along with radio silence and without navigation lights and our radar (for safety) was only reading contacts at three miles and beyond . . . . *Hermes* also has to turn into the wind to launch aircraft, which at that time was the opposite direction to the way the Fleet was heading. It was therefore impossible to stay in our station. We were either catching up on the Fleet or zonking back through them at a combined rate of 30 knots, while the whole Fleet was zigzagging, without lights or radar. It was difficult enough to keep track of all the contacts as they whizzed back and forwards across the radar screen (about 18 ships) but as they were lost within three miles, and zigzagging, we couldn't calculate their closest point of approach . . . . The first officer of the watch, looking out forward through the bridge windows for black, looming masses almost had a delayed nervous breakdown next morning.

We had three near misses, all of them passing nearer than a ship's length away. Two were frigates – which didn't really matter because we would have just sliced through them – and an oil tanker, which would have gone KABOOM. The tension was there all watch. Very exciting.

Only a couple of days till Bergen now, and after that only a couple of days until Portsmouth . . . .

*To Christine*                          HMS HERMES, *4 October 1979*

Our day yesterday was really quite exciting: I'm sure you would have enjoyed it. First, we marshalled aircraft. The handlers and directors are really keen on their job, and try to land the helicopters precisely, with the right wheel on the cross of the spot: necessary, because the parking is very packed. The Sea King helicopters that they use are really big and when you are marshalling the thrust from the rotors nearly knocks you over. The Petty Officer supervising me grabbed hold of me to keep me upright!

The Flight Deck handlers have a compartment in the island where they hang out, and rush out on to the freezing deck to handle the aircraft. Inside it is like the mutinous fo'c'sle on the *Bounty*. One bloke was shiftily and meticulously slitting a sheet of paper with a sheath knife many times. I didn't stay in there very long. When they grinned evilly they only had three teeth in their heads. Outside, on the Flight Deck, the handlers who stood around there were quite normal: but in this grotto they were quite evil.

My other experience that day was in Flyco [Flying Control] . . . . You have to know everything about the Flight Deck, all the refuelling points, electricity points, escape routes, fire points, where all the lights are, what all the lines mean, and how to operate flying: all the commands, wind direction and speed, control of aircraft, etc. He [the Lieut. Commander (F)] normally grills people on it, but he didn't bother with me as I'd extracted every last drop of information from the Leading Airman sitting in Flyco. I knew absolutely everything. Unfortunately, when he made me take charge of the flying I messed it up . . . . I was really tense all the time, and could easily have gone through to the end of their watch at 4 a.m. without feeling tired . . . . A carrier at night is really quite impressive, and this Lieut. Commander was really hankering after the old days. Every other word he said was "Fixed Wing". He . . . was longing for the days when *Invincible*, etc. would be roaming around. His arguments were based on the fact that he . . . had been in the navy since 1954 and flown with Nelson at Trafalgar, and I was some Midshipman So and So. However, I was quite happy for him to rattle on . . . . Anyhow, another day well spent, and one day nearer to you.

*To H and E*                                    HMS HERMES, *23 October 1979*

Here is the sheet showing the cottage that we are buying. It is really very appealing, and it is very kind of you to help us to buy a house which is appealing rather than practical!

We went to Clungunford on Saturday and spent the day walking around in the sunshine. It was beautifully quiet, with the birds singing, and we wandered down to the little river and saw the cottage nestling in the trees.

We also managed to get all the surveyors, solicitors, etc. going over the weekend; so it was very successful. We are now back at sea for three weeks and Christine is working hard at Camberley. It is all like Dartmouth there [the WRAC Officers Training School] but Christine dutifully gets up at 6.30 a.m. and dusts her room and bulls her shoes so she is on top of the system. She enjoys it, anyway . . . .

*To Christine*                      HMS HERMES, *24 October 1979*

I have emerged from the steamy depths to write to you. Working this hard is really exhausting . . . . All the engines are covered in beautiful brass dials and plates as they were made about twenty years ago up in Barrow in Furness. The steamies are proud of all these brass plates and keep them really bright. Of course, nowadays nothing is brass: all either painted metal for gauges or chrome plated steel for the plates. It's such a shame that when a ship has absolutely everything worked out – all the possible fittings you could want, all the guides to emergencies, and diagrams on each piece of machinery showing what each is and how it works – that the ship should be ending its life and then everything will be thrown away. All departments have been scavenging *Ark Royal* for spares to the machinery, as of course they don't make them any more.

The Sea Harriers are embarking today, and make quite a noise over our grot as the Flight Deck is our deckhead (ceiling).

*To Christine*                      HMS HERMES, *31 October 1979*

We had an excellent expedition to Snowdon yesterday . . . . All the sailors were really cheerful and put up with all the setbacks. At first, when the path was easy, they trotted along quite happily, clutching their four cans of beer each, just like kiddies with teddy bears. They ate their packed lunches by about 9 a.m. and had their cups of coffee and snacks at "Pete's Eats" at about 10 a.m. Off we rolled up the path, with all of them cheerily asking about when we were going to turn back. About three-quarters of the way up, the path just stops, and it is straight up some scree: only about a quarter of a mile long, but half the height of the mountain, very steep, and making us go on all fours most of the time. Once we had gone up it a little way it was obviously impossible to come down, so we carried on determinedly to the top. All the men got stuck in and went up without complaining at all. By this time the clouds were all over us, visibility was down to about ten yards, all the rocks were dripping wet, and the wind was up to sixty knots. It was really grim: climbing up in rushes between wind gusts, and clinging to the side of the hill when the wind came. One steward was hit smack on the head by a stone from all this scree being pushed down by our feet, and there was blood everywhere. He just had to lump it. If he'd been unconscious, we'd have just had to wait until he came round and then made him walk. There was no way we could have carried him up because our feet just couldn't find any firm ground.

Once we were at the top, we walked down the track of the mountain railway, and often had to kneel down or lie down because the wind was so strong. Jolly Jacks had a go at leaning into the wind and being bird men, flapping their arms and leaping up and down.

At the bottom we left the blokes in a pub (they deserved it) and walked back and hitched the six miles to where we had left the minibus. After a good cafe meal we drove back to Holyhead and had a good sing-song in the van. Excellent, I haven't sung so many songs since OTC days. At Holyhead we were messed around: had to cut short their drinking hour, went out to sea to try to get back to *Hermes*, but couldn't make it because of the storm. We were put in RAF VALLEY for the night . . . . Steve and myself were OK in the officers' mess and had a really good evening. The men were all taken into town and back to the pubs, so it wasn't too bad for them.

I really enjoyed the trip: just like OTC, and a really good bunch of blokes. A laugh all the way from start to finish. We eventually got back to *Hermes* at lunchtime today via helicopter.

*To E*                            HMS HERMES, *1 November 1979*

I'm glad to hear Mrs Brush is keeping you company while Hugh is away [in the United States]. It was very nice to get a long letter from you . . . . Glad to hear that your caterpillars are in such great demand, but if they are eating your veg they can be put off by spraying them with salt water.*

The other day we took some sailors off for an expedition up Snowdon. They were all very jolly and went up trailing strings of beer cans with them. When the going got rough they all knuckled down to it and were still very amusing and good natured. The wind was quite amazing at the top and often we just had to cling to the side of the hill, so it was all quite exciting.

Christine is getting on well at Camberley and should finish by the end of the month . . . . We must arrange for you to meet Christine's parents some time this Christmas when we get some leave. Perhaps you'd like to think of suitable dates . . . .

* The caterpillars were attacking our broccoli. A friend delightedly collected them for a nature study class.

*To Christine*                   HMS HERMES, *4 November 1979*

We had a good mess dinner last night: the best food I have tasted this cruise, with a really good civilian trials chap to talk to. We were having a fascinating discussion, ranging from freedom, to the class war, unborn babies, African tribal antagonisms, rehabilitation of prisoners, but some fish-head* Commander kept trying to butt in with things about the aircraft he used to fly, which ship he had commanded last, etc. My opinion of senior fish-head officers is still the same as it ever was: all utterly useless and without brains. After Commander, it's all the people who go to the right cocktail parties and are utterly stupid and shout at each other who get on. The intelligent ones leave . . . .

Anyway, it doesn't bother me cos I'm a pusser, and every Commander S is of course extremely intelligent. This morning

* Fish-head = Seaman branch.

we had a "feedback" session with our Training Officer, a
Lieut. Commander Fish-head, who kept on wanting to know
what watches we were keeping with various departments. He
even asked if we kept watch in the Supply Department. Mike
and I choked and spluttered: *watches* in the Supply Dept! When
he sees us crawling into breakfast after a night in the bar does
he imagine we are tired out through keeping the middle watch
in the vegetable store? . . . .

When is it you get told about your appointments? I hope
you get something that you like and something near Portsmouth or Chatham (what a tall order).* When I see you on
Friday I'll hear all the news.

* Christine was actually sent to Larkhill in Wiltshire: not too distant from
  Portsmouth.

*To Christine*                          HMS HERMES, *13 November 1979*

It's only a couple of days to go until I see you again, and the
time goes really quickly. Living a life of seeing each other at
weekends would be easy. It was so good being with you on
Sunday when we hadn't expected it. Every hour seemed
precious.

I caught the last train from Guildford, full of sleeping Jacks,
and got back in time to get plenty of sleep. Monday was pretty
hectic and included showing a party of schoolchildren around
*Hermes*. They ended up being grilled by the Captain on why
they weren't joining the Navy. Unfortunately, we had to
present the view of why the Navy was so good in yo-ho terms
– having responsibility, travelling and being at sea for months,
going through a tough selection test so only the best are picked
– in fact, all the things that make me cringe.

*To H and E*                            HMS NELSON, *December 1979*

We managed to move out from Birmingham successfully,
and everything has been going very well. It looks like we

should be able to avoid the closing order by doing the improvements very slowly over a number of years.*

I have now moved into *HMS Nelson*, Portsmouth, for our courses which will go on until August. Hope to see you at Christmas sometime.

* The County Council had threatened to apply a closing order which would have prevented Dave and Chris from occupying their cottage. They agreed to carry out the stipulated improvements (like putting in a damp course) and all was well.

*To Nigel Billington*                    HMS NELSON, *late February 1980*

You write such nice letters I can see why you get so many back. Very kind of you to ask about wedding presents – anything SMALL very much appreciated. (If no ideas, book/ record tokens very welcome). Swords will come from *Nelson*, so no problem there.*

Hope everything in Plymouth is going well . . . . Those lovely weekends all the time: hope you manage to get back from the West Country to see C. now and again.

By the way, would you mind being second-standby best man? My original best man is hacking his way through the jungles of South-East Asia from Hong Kong to UK and may or may not have been eaten by crocodiles en route. He usually arrives back after the thing which he specially came back from Hong Kong for is over.† My standby best man is fairly sound and reliable, but if he too is struck down, would you mind stepping in? (The chances of you actually having to step in are about 5 per cent.) Very decent of you Nigel (ho,ho). It doesn't involve any extra work for you; if it does happen it only involves standing at the front when everybody else is standing at the back, and I would give you a full speech saying who to thank, etc. Thank goodness you don't have any sordid childhood stories to tell!

* Nigel was to form one of the guard of honour outside the church.
† A canard: Chris Briggs arrived in plenty of time to take Dave out for a traditional last bachelor's evening.

*To H and E*                    *As From* HMS NELSON, PORTSMOUTH,
                                      [*Posted 3 March 1980*]

I hope Hornby is having some nice weather now, as we have
had some lovely days here already. It must be great walking
in the hills at this time of the year. We have been able to get
out into the South Downs for some afternoons at weekends,
which has been very pleasant, but of course there are always
so many people and screaming kids around!

Thank you for your nice long letters. I am very lazy in
writing back to you. I'm glad that Jonathan is hopeful of going
to Manchester as I'm sure Selly Oak would have driven him
potty (the present incumbent hasn't been there all that long).*
However, we both feel quite sad not to be living there any
more, as we had such a lovely time there.

I have now finished my Warfare courses and am on to the
Supply part before we go to Chatham after Easter. So, we have
now finished running over hills and shoring up simulated
damaged ship's compartments, etc. It's much more civilised
now!

Christine has been playing lots of tennis recently . . . . It is
what she joined for, and I'm sure she loves it . . . . All the
preparations for the wedding seem to be going fine. Christine's
father has even managed to get a vintage Rolls Royce for the
wedding car – really exciting!

Must finish now, as tomorrow I've got a hard day's work in
the main galley (back to *Intrepid* again: training never seems to
progress very much).

  * Jonathan's Bishop wanted him to take a Birmingham parish, and Selly
    Oak was among those suggested, but Helena and he both wanted to
    move north.


*To Nigel Billington*              HMS NELSON, *early March 1980*

I was really sad to hear about you and C. I know it is no
consolation, but every nice, kind-hearted man I've known has
been hurt by his girl-friend and him splitting up. It seems to
be one of those horrible things in life that the bad guys never
get hurt and the good guys do. I'm very sorry that it has
happened to you as well.

Things sound quite exciting in *Drake*: actual activity! Here in *Nelson* everything is very quiet, which suits me fine. Unfortunately, for the last three weeks I have been with L. and these poor demented Wrens just haven't been programmed to slope off (which is Tinker's only accomplishment in life). Consequently, DSO comes up to L. (who works in the office, seemingly, from 4 a.m. to 2359 every day, doing Sweet FA) demanding "Where is Tinker?" Tinker, being a sensible chap, is either in bed or has caught the 2.15 train to Salisbury: and who cares about a few slaps on the wrist when life is a three-hour working day?

Anyway, I'll look forward to hearing all the news from *Drake* at the wedding. See you then.


*To H and E*                    *As From* HMS NELSON, PORTSMOUTH,
                                   [*posted 14 March 1980*]


Thanks very much for a lovely weekend [Dave stayed with us, Saturday-Sunday, 8-9 March]. You always go out of your way to make a visit enjoyable, and it was really pleasant. I'm sorry that your spinning wheel doesn't have all the right bits, but it does look very nice.

PS.: Thanks very much for the birthday present, just received. It is very kind of you always to remember, but I never remember it myself and never celebrate it, so don't feel obliged to send one!


*To H and E*                    HMS PEMBROKE, CHATHAM,
                                   [*posted 8 May 1980*]


As usual, it takes ages to get a letter from me! Since coming to Chatham things have been very busy, with lots of homework and other naval delights. Our Course Officer likes to think of *Pembroke* as the University of the Navy. With rules like "Not allowed ashore before 5 p.m. without the Course Officer's permission", and an instruction that tells you to open an envelope before taking out the contents, it is much more like prep school.

Thank you so much for your kind present. It has helped us so much in making the cottage sound. The thatcher is going to come in July or August, and then the cottage will be in a much better state. Unfortunately, over the last twenty years it hasn't been looked after, and they just painted over or boarded over the rotten bits to forget them. It has been very exciting over the last three weekends as we have been down there, working away. We have taken out the old plaster-board panelling, chipped off plaster, and peeled off, wallpaper. The cottage is becoming lovelier all the time. It is a complete timber-frame cottage and will look very nice inside after we have peeled off the last of the wallpaper, treated it, and painted it. I can't understand how the builder, Rogers, wanted to hide all the nice beams behind horrid plasterboard panelling.*

One of the interesting things about taking down the plaster and paper is to discover, underneath, newspaper pages from the time the plaster, etc., was put up. We discovered the racing results of 1913 behind the door, the election results of 1886 stuffed in a plug in a beam, and a report of the repeal of the Corn Laws [1846], which I have kept, behind the plaster. I hope you will be able to drop in sometime to see the cottage, maybe on your way down to Little Hampden. From Clungunford to Little Hampden is a lovely drive across Oxfordshire and Herefordshire. When we work on the cottage we stay at Ludlow in the Church Inn, Buttercross, which is a very nice, friendly place . . . .

If you do visit the cottage [on your own] the floorboards upstairs have holes in, the main one being from the time before they had stairs and just had a ladder from the ground floor through a hole in the ceiling. Also, please test your footstep before you trust yourself to a plank.†

Anyway, things are progressing very well and apart from the thatching and the damp course we should be able to do the rest ourselves quite quickly . . . .

---

* At one time the cottage was owned by Mr Rogers, and the place was known locally as Rogers' Cottage. He had made some botched additions to the old fabric.

† Dave and Christine used the sound boards among those they found for the ceiling of one room, and made a completely new floor for the other room.

*To H and E*                          HMS PEMBROKE, CHATHAM,
                                           *2 June 1980*

It was very kind of you to offer to help us out again, financially, but at the moment we don't really need money, only time! As we have been working on the cottage we have realised that if we had let building firms do the jobs the character of the cottage would have been destroyed. And it really is a labour of love for us, as the cottage looks lovelier every week. For example, in the dining room we discovered under the concrete, a magnificent stone-flagged floor, and if we had let a building firm dig up the floor (to put in the damp course) the flags would have been destroyed by their pneumatic drills.

Anyway, it is all progressing and it should be ready by August. Please don't think you haven't helped us as much as Jonathan or Mark because without your help in leaping in with assistance, no matter what the risks were, the chance would have slipped by and I am sure we wouldn't have found such a lovely place ever again.

Fortunately, we'll be able to get to Jonathan's induction.* It is in the period of my exams, but the Navy has been kind enough to let me go when everyone else will be working into the evening on Friday. Christine's parents are also coming . . . .

By the way, if you are interested in a timber framed thatched cottage, there is one going for auction at Hopton Heath just two miles away from us . . . . It's to be auctioned . . . at Ludlow. I'll send you the details when I'm next in Ludlow during shopping hours (on 21 June).†

* Jonathan was installed as Rector of Stretford, Manchester, on 20 June. Dave and Chris arrived with about two minutes to spare before the service was due to start. Actually Jonathan had given instructions that it would *not* begin until he was told of their safe arrival.
† Dave's enthusiasm for cottages rather ran away with him!

*To H and E*                          HMS PEMBROKE, CHATHAM,
                                           *1 July 1980*

It must be very nice to be back at Little Hampden now, if a bit damp. I'm sure Mrs Brush is having a great time with the mice.

It was very kind of you to lug the coins into the bank [Dave's famous collection] . . . . You may be relieved to know that we have now obtained insurance from Lloyds for the cottage (through the good old White Ensign Association) . . . .

We have now heard solid rumours about our appointments and I am to be Captain's Secretary of *Glamorgan*, a sister ship to *Fife* . . . . She comes out of refit in December and it should be an exact re-run of our Middies' time in *Fife*, doing the same things we did then – trials in the Channel, followed by the dreaded Portland work-up, followed by a trip abroad. She is late, already, in her refit and may be later still. She is at Portsmouth, so it will be very easy to see Christine [at Larkhill] until *Glamorgan* starts going to sea. At long last at twenty-three I shall actually be earning my living [i.e. doing an executive job]. It will certainly be hard work. Anyway, we are to finish here at the end of the month and maybe we shall see you during August if we manage to get the cottage finished . . . .

*To H and E*                                     HMS PEMBROKE, CHATHAM,
                                                            *27 July 1980*

Hope the work at the moment is going well and that they [the FCO] are letting you look at everything after their security clearance. At the moment we are all going through "positive vetting" (sounds very clinical) where we are interviewed endlessly about everything under the sun.

Christine is now fully recovered and is fighting fit and back to playing tennis . . . . Last week we were lifting the flagstones in the dining room at the cottage so that we can dig out the earth underneath [before laying the damp course], and we ran into great difficulties with a family of fieldmice. There was an elaborate nest under the flags and we thought they were all inside so we put the nest in the garden. Unfortunately, Mummy was out, and came back later, so we had to search in the garden and bring the babies back inside, one by one, and put them at the mousehole entrance where they were grabbed and hauled inside. We only found the last of them next morning, and at first I thought he was dead, but he soon revived in the warmth of my hand and we fed him warm milk and made him a cosy nest in tissue paper and a sock. He was a sweet little thing and sat up on his hind legs washing his whiskers when we fed him milk. He would run around making little squeaking noises and curl up in his nest with his tail tucked underneath him. At the end of that day we left him in a nest made out of tissue paper and a bottle-cap full of milk by the mousehole for his mother to collect him. It would have been nice to hand-rear him if we had been staying at the cottage but, as it was, it would have been impossible to take him to *Pembroke* or Larkhill.

My new Captain has just written a very nice letter asking both Christine and myself to dinner and saying lots of welcoming things. He does seem a thoroughly agreeable man: what a relief. But of course, as all Captains are, he is a perfectionist. But as long as he is pleasant when he shouts at me it will make all the difference.

We are having difficulties at the moment persuading any builders' merchants to sell us concrete. In Shropshire, things are done on a haphazard basis so we are going to have to bring in some builders to do the job [of installing a damp course]. Unfortunately, we are a bit short of cash . . . .

PS.: Thanks very much for your nice letter from a few weeks ago.

*To H and E*                     WYKE REGIS, WEYMOUTH,
                                      *1 September 1980*

It was very nice to receive your long letters today: it took some time for them to reach me. I join *Glamorgan* in a fortnight, and they didn't know my address to send the letters on. I have just started a course (yet another!) at Portland, so that I can wave the bats at the helicopter to marshal it to land, or take off. It takes the army one day to train a soldier to do it; but we like to do things thoroughly, so here it takes two weeks.

As there is not enough room in the Wardroom for us, we all stay in this hotel in Weymouth, all kitted out with service furniture. It is just like being on holiday, and there are plenty of tourists still in Weymouth from all the industrial cities – I may even see my Selly Oak neighbours (they always come here).

It is very good news from Little Hampden. The *Times Literary Supplement* review [of H's last book] was very good, and you must be pleased that at last it is being covered by so many journals. Working at the moment on Mountbatten's papers must be fascinating and providing an interesting insight into the workings of the Navy. It must be very satisfying to be working on the sources again, rather than hammering ideas into the brains of first year students . . . . I was sorry to hear about Mrs Brush's mouth ulcer [our cat: she was soon cured] described in the letter you wrote to Christine. But I am sure she enjoys her liver (she had probably planned it).

We had a lovely time at the cottage in August, and we had three weeks together, which was quite remarkable. It is amazing how long everything takes to do: especially chasing around getting materials delivered. Of course, it helps immeasurably having the Mini, but her limit is one bag of plaster. We have now attended to the cracks on the front outside wall and rendered it over with cement to give a nice finish when it is painted white (covering the bricks). We have laid the floors for upstairs [replacing some of the ancient floor boards] and are plastering the panels inside [the downstairs rooms] between the wooden frames. The damp course has been laid for the stone floor, but we have had to leave the tiled floor as it was impossible to take the tiles up without breaking them and we could not have found replacements. Things are on the way up now . . . . It is very kind of you to keep helping us out . . . . Our thatcher is very difficult to keep nagging at, as he is never at home, but we are hopeful to have it done by Christmas. We have been top of his list since June.*

We met my new Captain, Captain Barrow, in August, as he kindly invited us to lunch and gave us some veggy from his vegetable garden to take back with us. He'd grown some huge parsnips. He is a very kind, pleasant man and very interested in people and easy to get on with, as well as (of course) demanding high standards: which is only right from a senior Captain. I could not have wished for a better Captain to work for, and I came away from lunch feeling very cheered.

Christine also had a very good time at the Army championship and had a nail-biting final match . . . . It was very exciting and a very even match but now Christine is the Army champion and came away with literally a bag full of cups and trophies.

Hope you have a nice time in Italy.

* The thatcher did not do the job by Christmas, but see the letter dated 14 March 1981.

*To H and E*         HMS GLAMORGAN, *28 November 1980*
*[posted, Portsmouth]*

It was very nice to receive your letter yesterday, full of good news. It would be lovely to see you at Clungunford over the Christmas holidays. We'll be there from 20th December until 4th January. Bring your walking clothes and binoculars. There's a lovely hill, that you can see from the front windows of the cottage, which has some beautiful views of Clungunford on one side in one valley and Clunbury on the other side, with valleys leading off into the distance. Clunbury looks very cosy from the hill with its solid, square, stone church tower and the village houses clustered around it. Incidentally, next to Clunbury church is an old L.N.W.R. railway carriage, dating from about 1910, being used as a garden shed.

The cottage has been coming along quite well, with one room finished now. It's amazing how much time it has all taken. Unfortunately, when you come, you won't be able to see much of the room as it will be full of furniture. We're going to stack all the furniture in there while we work on the other rooms.* The thatcher has been delayed by another month because somebody's cottage caught fire and so they are homeless (or very wet) until he can repair their thatch. However, he should start in mid-January.

Everything in *Glamorgan* is going well and it is very busy. Captain Barrow is a very human, lively and Christian gentleman, and very easy to work for. He is also very tolerant! He must get a bit fed up with having to "break in" a new Secretary every time (this is his third ship) and it is strange that if he

* At this time, Christine and David were living upstairs, right under the sloping rafters. With their Calor gas heater going, and their oil lamp they were, like Mr John Dormouse, "very snug".

were a Rear Admiral he would have a Commander as a Secretary and if he were in command of a shore establishment he'd have a Lieutenant-Commander! Still, I have a very helpful Commander S (Supply) who leaps into action at a moment's notice when I have got it totally wrong. Also, the Chief Writer in the office has years of experience behind him and even managed to find a SECRET file that I had lost: just after about ten seconds' thought.

I am now a Lieutenant, having finally made it. It is a great relief not to be training any more. We have ten Mids and Subs training on board and I think they are having quite a good time. *Glamorgan* is a very happy ship and completely opposite to *Fife*.

Christine is now a Lieutenant as well and stands a good chance of being a Captain in June. That's even faster than a pip a year. I think she is really looking forward to her next job as she's been at Larkhill for a year now and feels she has *done* that job. They are trying to find her somewhere near Portsmouth (or at any rate in the South East) which is good of them. When I saw my Appointer the other day and said I would do any job as long as it was in Portsmouth (which is by far the Navy's biggest base) his first question was: "How about Plymouth?" They don't change. Anyway, I think there is a good chance of being in Portsmouth for the next five years which is very hopeful.

I'm glad that you [E] are spinning and playing the organ as well: it must be lovely. We look forward to seeing you at Clungunford.

*To H and E*                                    4, CHURCH ROW, CLUNGUNFORD,
                                                    *27 December 1980*

Thank you for the lovely presents. They were very thoughtful, and quite original. It was a most amazing present to have a jigsaw of people you actually recognize when spreading out the pieces!* We put your presents into immediate use, making the jigsaw straight away and then putting on your gloves to go for a walk. On the way, a frenzied game-keeper came haring after us in his Land Rover thinking we were saboteurs of the Boxing Day shoot!

It was lovely to see you down here for Monday and Tuesday and we were thrilled that you could stay for so long. Hopefully, you will eventually be able to stay in the cottage without discomfort. We have just started working on the cottage again after taking three days off for Christmas. We decorated the cottage with holly and streamers and found that the Forestry Commission had kindly been cutting down huge Christmas trees for telegraph poles and there were plenty of tops about, which provided an ideal tree to take home.

* David's mother had taken a photograph at the wedding of them stepping into the vintage Rolls Royce which took them off to the reception. She found that Woolworths were able to enlarge amateur photos and turn them into jigsaw puzzles. Also she was then spinning wool regularly: she knitted David and Christine 'Unisex' gloves. On our visit she popped these gifts into their stocking.

*To H and E*　　　　　　　　HMS GLAMORGAN, *14 March 1981*
　　　　　　　　　　　　　　　　　　　　*[posted, Portsmouth]*

It was very kind of you to think of buying a birthday present, and very absorbing it is too [*The History of Myddle*: another Shropshire parish]. There were two men from his parish who were killed at Hopton Castle about two miles away [from Clungunford] in the Civil War, although why they were there, forty miles away in such a small castle, is a mystery.

I was very sorry to hear about Hugh's flu and bang on the head into the bargain; it must have been quite wretched . . . . I am sure you will have a marvellous time [after retirement] whether it is writing books, staying at Little Hampden or travelling abroad; I should think you have started to make plans already.

It sounds a lovely time that you had with Jonathan and Helena [at the Leighton Moss Bird Sanctuary] – seeing so many unusual birds. I hope that they had a good rest. Life must be very demanding in Manchester. I heard from Mark the other day . . . . Apparently it's very cold [in Liverpool] so he is coming to collect his blankets from Clungunford [Mark had been staying in his brother's cottage].

It has been quite a busy time on board, setting everything to work after the ship's three year refit (costing £50 million: no expense spared on the defence budget!!) We have already had two weeks of Portland at the beginning of February and we go back for our full work-up in May and the first part of June. NATO summer exercises follow on, where we practise escorting troop convoys across the Atlantic, and after that we go to the Persian Gulf from October to March to join the Americans (who presumably are there either to "protect" Pakistan's coastline, attack Iran's smouldering oil terminal, or generally fight the Russians). *Of course the dates that we are on patrol should not be talked about.* That unfortunately ruins our chances of escorting the Yacht during the Royal Honeymoon [in the Med].

Sea time tends to get in the way of seeing Christine (so tennis and hockey enjoy not being interrupted by husbands) but we have been very lucky with our leave, as Chris has managed to wangle a week off work while I am on leave in March.

The cottage has now been rethatched and looks very cosy. We stood outside, admiring the thatcher's work most of last weekend. He also left behind some very good wattles which will come in handy. The old straw which he removed is just like compost, so it's amazing that it lasted for so long. One room is now all neat and tidy* and we have removed the surplus furniture, and so "Stage I" is well under way.

The mice have a grand time while we are away: especially in the packing cases where they ate all the plastic armies in my *Diplomacy* game. They also ate their way through the plastic side of a 'Pot Noodle' and devoured the dehydrated contents inside. The sheep are getting woollier all the time and when they have been let out into the big fields they have terrific games with us and try to terrorise Christine by standing up against her: incredibly, they are about 4 feet 6 inches when

---

* This is the inner living room with its white plastered walls and bare beams and flagged floor. The furniture is simple – a large book case, a chest of drawers, a table, a piano, and a comfortable wooden high-backed arm chair. The view over the meadow to the river Clun is seen through the leaded panes of the old window.

upright.* A mad pheasant has taken to roosting in the tree by our window and makes us both jump when he suddenly lets out a great squawk at sunset and leaps up into his tree.

Hope to see you in the summer, sometime, we shall probably be here (at Clungunford) for most of August.

* In the little orchard just above the cottage two lambs were pastured. David and Christine fed them with biscuits bought specially for the lambs, but by this time they had grown up.

*To Christine*                    HMS GLAMORGAN, *28 June, 1981*
                                                          *At Kiel*

We have had a very busy time here at Kiel over the last week, with Captain's Secretaries rushing around at great speed and, fortunately, this time managing to avoid the wrath of their Captains . . . . Judging from the pace here I don't think you would particularly relish a trip to Mombasa. I have been working till 11 p.m. every day, but managed to get out on Friday afternoon (the Captain had the afternoon off to go shopping and the liaison officer invited us out for a trip and dinner in the afternoon). However, I nearly came unstuck because at Friday lunchtime the Captain had said to me that he wanted a long important letter about two officers' recommendations for university to be typed and despatched by Saturday at the latest. Knowing that he was going away on Saturday to Lübeck and wouldn't be in . . . I said "Aye Aye Sir" and doubled away smartly. However, at 0900 when I went in to the office on Saturday, Mr Hitchens told me that the Captain had come on board and wanted to see me. With my heart in my mouth I went up to see him; but fortunately he had just come to write another letter, and didn't mention the other.

For the rest of the time it has been impossible to get away. I had hoped to be able to go on a day-trip, guided tour, slap-up meal, etc. to Lübeck but *that* was the day the Captain decided to try a stoker for a crime which needed a punishment warrant (and a covering letter to be written, which explains it all) which is a mammoth operation to get off in three hours. Also, that day we had our first casualty [i.e. an accident case] which entails signals being written and rushing around and organising a ship's investigation.

The other time I tried to escape was when the liaison officer took us out, by request, to see the Open-Air Museum on the other side of Kiel which has a collection of reconstructed, thatched timber-framed farmhouses and barns, plus a wind-mill. It looked delicious from the outside, but when we tried to go in we found it had been closed half an hour before (the story of our lives!). Altogether, I only managed to spend ten Marks in Germany . . . .*

Anyway, tomorrow we sail for England – eventually – and go through the Kiel Canal, cut straight across the countryside. It should be very good as the country still has its small fields and rows of trees for hedgerows, even though extra-horrid square, modern box-type houses are springing up every-where . . . .

I've now got some details of when I am free for weekends in July as the duty list has just been published. Fortunately, this first weekend in July is free, but there is some doubt as to whether we will get in or not, depending on whether we can complete our trials for Seaslug. Yes, we are still doing trials! We should be thankful we're not doing foreign visits, work-up, exercises, potential officers', and dockyard families' visits AND TRIALS all at once . . . . It really all depends on whether we get some clear sunny days to track these aircraft doing their tight twisting turns – so I can't really give any estimates of the chances of getting in . . . .

One of the other good bits of news is that I've ordered four crates of wine . . . . I can't really remember what they taste like because my palate was fairly well gone by the end of the wine-tasting session (as well as the rest of me, which is probably why I ordered four crates) . . . .

Unfortunately the chance of a job in Chatham at the moment looks pretty slim. Mind you, I would love to be part of the staff who are closing it down. I would raze the Supply School to the ground and dance around the flames! . . . It is really rather sad that, after we have all worked ourselves to death, with goodness knows how many late nights of "fix-its" and "buck-ups" to meet each deadline to get *Glamorgan*

* Ironically, the *Lancashire Evening Post* (15 July 1981) printed a photograph of David with the headline ROCK AHOY FOR DAVE saying what a great time he had at Kiel, "riding on the crest of a wave". Presumably all dreamed up by some Navy PR man.

operational and functional after refit – which has taken a whole year to achieve – that two years later the whole thing will just be scrapped. Talk about the futility of human life! All it will have been for will be – a couple of officers' promotions, ratings fulfilling their mandatory sea time, and for the rest – a lot of hard work, separations, and pains in the neck.

Everybody would have had a lot more enjoyable, cushy time if they had left us in refit for a couple of years longer. It would have cost the country far less: e.g. £60,000 per week in fuel, and £10,000 per trip for each of the hundreds (literally) of aircraft sorties that were flown for radar tracking. The sensible thing is [would be] that once a ship has been built it will stay that way, and not have bits and pieces added on, in expensive refits. Hopefully, we will run our ships into the ground and then scrap them, rather than (as now) keeping them in perfect order (terribly expensive) until the day they die.

*To Christine*                    HMS GLAMORGAN, *28 July 1981*

Thank you for your very nice letter which I received yesterday. I am glad that everything was quiet on your night at the cottage . . . . As usual, these letters from me aren't full of good news, and I am afraid I have been made duty [officer] on the Saturday of 1 August. I didn't think that as I was duty on the Friday I'd also have to do Saturday. But it's happened . . . . I hope that you will be free on the weekend 7-9 August to go to the cottage? I went last weekend, having successfully bought a folding bike at Woolworths (my favourite shop) for only £39.95p . . . . It doesn't go very fast (about 6 m.p.h.) but it does its job very well, and of course all the downhill bits are "free". The long hill down towards Onibury is super. On board ship, it sits in my wardrobe very happily, and the clothes hang above it. At Clungunford, I borrowed your bike to go to Craven Arms. It's so whizzy. I also had a very nice cycle ride around up to Obley and Pentre Hodrey and all around the hills just before Clun. It was a brilliant day, and I started off, thinking, "I must get Christine to come cycling, cos it's such lovely coutryside, and you miss so much in the car". But when I came back feeling very tired and sore after so many hills I had second thoughts! Maybe I'll get you to come as far as Hopton Castle before the hills start.

Must go now for more duty.


*To Christine*                    HMS GLAMORGAN, *4 September 1981*

I received some good news when I returned. Captain Barrow has been up to see Captain Douds, the Supply Appointer, and has pressed him to appoint me to Chatham! Also, my appointment here is going to finish much earlier, in April. I may have to do the Greenwich course first . . . but that's only an hour away on the London-Strood line . . . .* It is not certain that they will find me a job there, but I should say the chances are 80 per cent rather than 10 per cent as before. So, if it all comes about, it makes the situation look very rosy. Presumably a job at Chatham would last until February 1984 in the normal course . . . . On the weekend when we come back from Amsterdam I will come and see you at Chattenden [barracks] . . . . On the weekend October 2-4 I have volunteered for duty as I believe you will be on duty . . . and then I hope we can go to Clungunford for those last two weekends, 9-11 and 16-18 October.

It was very sad when we had to say goodbye to each other on Monday. It always seems a waste to have to go back to work, but somehow now with the chance of coming to Chatham it doesn't seem half so bad. Because I love you, lots and lots, and can't wait for the time when we can live together . . . .

* Strood: the railway station for Rochester where Christine and David hoped to live together in married quarters at last.


*To Christine*                   HMS GLAMORGAN, *25 October 1981*

We are spending this weekend at Gibraltar, which has fortunately not been too demanding. I am always duty [officer] when all the functions occur, and being Secretary and Gibraltar liaison[officer] fit in quite easily. I have now added to my record of missing our Admiral's departure in Portsmouth by missing the Governor's departure from the Captain's dinner last night. He wasn't amused; but it's amazing how he becomes quite pleasant again the next morning!

When I left you at Strood I felt very sad, and still do from time to time. Church service especially reminds me of being with you at Clungunford. Everything seems very far away at the moment, even though we are only about as far away as Scotland. I arrived back in Portsmouth at about midnight on the Sunday. Everything was very still and autumnal. The basin was completely smooth, and *Bulwark*'s great mass was totally mirrored in it, in the light of the great arc lamps to one side of the dockyard. Some drunken sailors staggered ahead of me, about two hundred yards away to *Glamorgan*, and the dockyard steam was hissing in the leaks in its pipes.

Our send-off itself from Portsmouth was quite poignant. It was a blustery day, yet Flag Officer Portsmouth himself braved the weather and drove along beside us in his barge, waving us goodbye and seeing us off. The round tower at the entrance to Portsmouth harbour was absolutely crammed at the top with families waving us goodbye: all wrapped up in their coats against the wind.

However, we haven't had much chance to feel sad this last week. Our workaholic masters have been keeping us very busy: so busy in fact, that it was almost impossible to find a half-hour slot when the Captain and various divisional officers would be free to do Requestmen. Even at Portland we weren't that pushed: and this is self-imposed. There has been quite a lot of grumbling in the ship, complaining that we are working too hard. For the Wardroom film nights, when the W/R is usually packed out, there were only four or five watching, out of fifty. However, I can't imagine there will be any change . . . .

The weather, of course, is lovely now. On the first day at sea (spent at Portland!) it was turgid, and the second day it was worse (Bay of Biscay). About 2.30 p.m. on Wednesday when I was on the Flight Deck it started to brighten up. It has been lovely and warm since; not too hot, with a nice breeze blowing. Saturday in Gibraltar was quite horrid at first: very wet, and the light outside was strangely dark.

Today, Sunday, has been a glorious day. I went with the Captain and Gerry Hunt (the Flight Commander) to a curry lunch at the house of the washing-machine man (Captain

Paul). He lives in the house where Nelson's body was stored while *Victory* was being repaired at Gibraltar. His living room is reputed to have been the place where he "popped out" of his barrel because of the gasses blowing the lid off. (On Thursday we passed over the scene of the battle, had a short service, and laid a wreath. At least it was warm for their battle: unlike our visit to *Victory* last weekend.)

Tomorrow we sail from Gibraltar and go back into blue uniform (it's jolly confusing) having worn our whites for three days. It was quite sad for the long-serving Captains at the curry lunch as they were saying that they had just worn their whites for the last time in their careers (all of them were being cut by the defence cuts). They were trying to decide if they could stain the uniforms and wear them as plain clothes . . . .

My next letter should be from Naples next week. Mail is only being delivered at each port until we get to the Gulf (but we are not there long) so it won't come very often.

*To H and E*                    HMS GLAMORGAN, *7 November 1981*
                                            *At Aqaba*

You will probably be quite surprised to hear from me – and to learn that I am in Jordan of all places! As it is some time since I wrote to you, and having been goaded by your S.A.E.* I can't remember if I told you that *Glamorgan* was due to deploy to the Persian Gulf to form part of the patrol that is "protecting" oil tankers – [which] all started since the Russians invaded Afghanistan. Anyway, here we are on the way out. Aqaba is about the size of Kirkby Lonsdale, surrounded by some terrific barren sandstone hills, but somehow [it] seems to be quite important. There are a dozen merchant ships anchored in the bay (as there is no jetty), all doing very little. But presumably as this is Jordan's only port most of Jordan's goods come this way. We are here for the weekend only before taking over the patrol.

Last weekend we were in Naples and I managed to see Pompeii: most impressive, as all the buildings are still about

---

* His mother, having written three letters and received no reply, sent David a stamped addressed envelope as a broad hint.

fifteen feet high . . . . It is quite strange to walk on a Roman street whose paving stones are still smoothly joined together, showing the two distinct cartwheel ruts which run down the street (avoiding the stepping stones) made 1,900 years ago. Compared to the decay most of our castles have suffered, Pompeii has done very well!

We are due to visit Mombasa and Karachi on our travels and return to Portsmouth at the end of February. I think my next job will be in Chatham (despite the cuts) which if it happens will be very welcome.

Depending on when you plan to travel to India, I might see you there. I hope that "retired" life is treating you [H] well. I can't imagine that your work will be any less . . . . Do you plan to stand for the Morecambe Liberals again at the next General Election? It would certainly be a satisfying end to your political career if you could be an MP in the first Liberal Government for fifty years – which certainly looks on the cards now: even if (as I do) you can't stand the SDP.

I hope the organ playing is coming along well and that you [E] are playing for weddings as well as funerals! The organ in our little village church has just had an overhaul and during the activities to raise funds it was discovered what an excellent instrument it was, and how the Archbishop of York came to consecrate it in 1894. Not bad for a parish (now) of 253 on the electoral roll.

Things have been progressing well at the cottage. We have now dismantled the conservatory at the back (it went to the people next door) and have dug down, built stone foundations, and restored the back wall (removing all the horrid Hindenburg-line concrete blocks), finally painting it black and white on our last weekend there. There is still so much to be done, but it is all coming along. We now have our beams from the barn that we obtained "on site", all ready to use.* Quite how we are going to build with them is more difficult. It took five of us to lift the main tie-beams.

All for now, from a very hot November out here in our tropicals!

* David had bought the beams of an old barn, being pulled down. He and Christine planned to re-erect them as the framework for an extension to their cottage.

*To Christine*　　　　　HMS GLAMORGAN, *9 November 1981*
*At Aqaba*

The time seems to be going very slowly, although the days pass quickly enough. It's only three weeks ago that we were together, but it seems (to everyone on board) ages since we left. Roll on the next fifteen weeks. Our programme from now on is less of a Mediterranean cruise and more like being in the Navy: three weeks at sea, then Bahrein for the weekend 28 November-1 December, and then another three weeks before Mombasa . . . .

Having the Admiral on board has in fact made life easier (he keeps the Captain busy). For once, my [official] thank you letters weren't totally rewritten. I think the Admiral is much more keen on the operational side than on paperwork, which is a great relief. The Flag Lieutenant and Staff officers keep him fed with paper . . . .

Let me tell you how things have been going since Naples . . . . On Wednesday we passed close by Libya (uneventfully, fortunately) and went through the Russian anchorage off the coast there near an inlet called Mersa Sullom. There were about eight ships of frigate/destroyer size, and most of their ships' company stood on deck, looking at us (as we did). It must be very boring for them, stuck in the middle of nowhere.

On Thursday night we came through the Suez Canal. At Port Said (the northern end) a whole host of small traders and officials gathered round us, all on the scrounge for cigarettes or whatever. The official documents were an amazing hotchpotch. They required all the old certificates, such as one certifying that the ship was free of rats, had a boat's crew ready, etc. They wanted crew-lists, details of the double bottoms, cargo, etc.: but if we could not supply the information they were not particularly bothered. I signed all the ship's documents for the Captain: I don't really know *what* I signed. They just put lots of papers under my nose and said "Sign here, please", and so I did. After all, they will never get back to you, will they? I enjoyed myself, anyway.

A "Gully Gully man" came on board as well. He is a magician who makes coins appear in people's hands, chickens in people's shirts, etc. He did a show in the Wardroom where the Admiral, Captain, Commander and Staff Officers were his main targets. I think the poor Admiral was quite embarrassed having to say "Veroomshka-keroomshka". The Suez Canal is really where a different world begins. At night, Port Said was full of lights and little boats and a warm "eastern", slightly sweaty smell, with people jabbering away in a totally strange language . . . . By day it was strange to see on the right (Egyptian) side that the country was fertile with palm trees and green vegetation whereas on the left it was totally barren: not a sausage. It was just like pictures of the moon, completely lifeless . . . . There were still signs of the earthworks thrown up by the Israelis and Egyptians when they faced each other over the canal; remains of gun emplacements and trenches; plenty of barbed wire up the banks. The houses over fifteen years old had gaping, large, shell holes and bullet pock-marks in them. In the canal itself were the remains of where the Egyptians had simply bull-dozed earth into the canal and then driven their columns over the top. And everywhere there was still tons of iron debris: pipes, pontoon bridges, entanglements, the odd landing craft and truck: all heaped on the banks. In the Great Bitter Lakes you could see in the distance the old hulls of ships that were marooned [in the 1956 war] sticking up out of the water, some with bows out in the air, some just with masts sticking up, and others looking quite normal – just settled down.

The shipping that actually goes through the canal is of course quite small. Most of them look like the Second World War type of merchant ship – we made for a very old-fashioned convoy, going through.

Once we had reached Suez at the bottom end of the canal, everything changed abruptly again. The Gulf of Suez, and Gulf of Aqaba, are very grand and rugged. A great biblical landscape with ridged, bumpy sandstone mountains and cliffs running bare down to the sea. They do look very imposing: but it is really a country with nothing in it at all! . . .

On Sunday we went on a super beach picnic [at Aqaba] and had a whale of a time. The coral in the water is very sharp, though, and it looked a bit like a battlefield afterwards; with people bleeding variously. I have got grazed knees just from brushing the coral with my shorts, and look rather like a schoolboy.

Amazingly, we managed to pick up the service from the Cenotaph at 11 o'clock, and had our two minutes' silence on the beach: not far from where Lawrence came down to take Aqaba with his Arab legion. With those stark hills and the bright blue sky and the sand, yet with the rain coming down in London, it emphasised what a total war [1914-1918] was, and how far everyone came to take part in it. I think we are going to have our service on the 11th at 11 o'clock, which will be fitting. During the two minutes' silence I thought how you would be doing the same as we were, and it brought you very close. It is the one time of the year that I can always remember exactly where I was. Last year, Larkhill, and before that at Guildford station before coming to see you at Camberley. And so on. It has a certain quality about it that is very much tied up with the Autumn.

The Captain has now come back on board, which has ruined my concentration . . . (change of pen, as I have retreated to my cabin from the office to avoid the last-minute little jobs he loves giving me). Before I go down to do a rush-letter he wants typed, suddenly, just before the mail closes in half an hour . . . I have got time for a last paragraph: this letter was going to be much longer . . . .

*To Christine*                    HMS GLAMORGAN, *16 November 1981*

I have just been reading your letters again, which fill me with a lovely warm glow and sense of happiness. The time between now and February becomes slowly but steadily less: it's now almost a month since we sailed, and yesterday the 20 per cent mark [of time] passed: next weekend it will be the quarter way through mark. Not much, but it steadily goes.

Life is really very nice now. The Captain is totally occupied by the Admiral, the work can be done at a normal pace, and I can even get my head down in the afternoon! Just like *Hermes* again . . . .

In our travels we have now left the Red Sea, which became very hot (115 degrees F on deck and 171 degrees next to the boiler). We are proceeding, roughly, along the bottom of Saudi Arabia, but into the Indian Ocean a bit, which is very pleasant:

warm, but with a breeze blowing, which lets the air-conditioning work properly and the evaporators work better (which make our water from sea-water). Incidentally, our water costs 30p per gallon: £5,500 on fuel is spent every day making it! It would be almost as cheap to bathe in gin.

The other day I had a day in a French frigate operating out of Djibouti. They live very well there and the ship was amazingly clean and cool. The bit I liked best was the French windows and verandah which they had in the Wardroom. They were very patient with our French and didn't even correct our "Franglais" (we had all read the column in *Punch* avidly before going, to get up to flying speed). Thoroughly boozed up we returned on board and I spent the rest of the afternoon in bed sleeping it off. It was a most impressive frigate, bristling with guns and looking very steady and warlike . . . .

*To Christine*         HMS GLAMORGAN, *21 November 1981*

Things have been very exciting here today. Feelings among the ratings have been getting rather bad – i.e. too many exercises. We have exercised almost continuously since we left Portsmouth, and no fun at all. The patrol we are on is called *Armilla*, which they dubbed "Armpits" (*Armilla* = Portland in the Sun!). Self-inflicted work-up is very hard to justify. Anyway, the Master at Arms went to the Commander and told him . . . that a mutiny would be taking place in about one hour's time unless things changed! As he went to leave, he found a poem had been pinned to the Commander's door . . . which proved the point. The result of all this is that at last . . . the Captain and Commander have decided that the ship will have a day's fun next week (between exercises) . . . . Personally, I'm enjoying life immensely, and I wish the Admiral would stay on to keep the Captain busy. At the moment my sun-tan is coming along beautifully. I watch every Wardroom film and have time to write to you; I have actually started all my paperbacks and I have as much sleep as I like. What could be better? Even the stewards have settled down now and stopped grumbling about life. Work takes about an hour or two per day. Unfortunately, of course, once the ship starts having fun, and the Captain can start giving out little jobs instead of receiving them, "my Secretary" will once again be running hither and thither on paltry errands. Never mind – we have now reached the "Quarter Way Through" point . . . .

Also, today came the news that we are thinking of arriving in Portsmouth on 26 February so that we can unload two Seaslugs in Plymouth, rather than in April (the timing of this announcement is amazing) . . . .

*22 November 1981*

I received two nice letters today from 7th and 9th November. You really seem to be busy at the moment: it makes me feel quite guilty . . . . Your girls seem to be keeping you busy. Mine [Dave's Division] are into debt and babies at the moment, but it is a passing fad . . . . I enjoyed reading the cutting on the medieval builder . . . . Just wait until I start on our moat and gatehouse. I saw that he was building a "medieval" cavity wall, so I suppose he had to conform to building regs: but he has managed to include a timber frame in the design, which is clever. Maybe that's what we'll have to do.

Not much news of the ship. We are still off the top, right-hand point of Saudi Arabia, about one hundred miles out to sea. I didn't realise how close to India Saudi Arabia actually is. Also, Saudi Arabia seems to be just as big! We have just finished an exercise with the US Navy (in which we were sunk) and after entertaining all the Captains on Monday and the Sultan of Muscat on Tuesday and various others on Wednesday (Sultan of Oman?) we sail for Bahrein where we are spending the weekend, and some more mail should go off and come on. This letter should be despatched from Muscat on 25 November. After Bahrein, we actually start our patrol – for two weeks, until we sail for Mombasa. It is quite cool here, now, inside the ship and gently warm outside on deck: enough to keep the suntan going.

*To Christine*          HMS GLAMORGAN, *25 November 1981*

For a couple of days now I have been thinking that there was something special about 25 November . . . . I now know what it was, and maybe you will have read something in the papers by the time you read this. Today we wrote off both propellers and are now "powerless". And all for anchoring too close to the shore in a pretty spot which was charted to be deep enough. How we are going to get home we don't quite know.

We went over a shallow sandstone rock and the ship was bodily lifted up on its shafts, which are now buckled: and great chunks have been taken out of the propellers. The gear-mountings in the ship were bodily lifted up inside the ship, but the exact damage is not known. If the gearing is distorted it may not be worth replacing them (£8 million) and so *Glamorgan* will be scrapped. If the gearing is OK then the Navy can send out two new propellers and shafts from England and refit us in dry dock, either at Abu Dhabi, Mombasa, or Karachi (if they can take us). Or else two tugs will come out from Gibraltar and tow us round to Portsmouth via South Africa (about 10,000 miles, which at 8 knots under tow will take about 50 days' sailing). Presumably C-in-C Fleet will send out a team of experts to assess what is to be done and the MOD will decide on our fate.

Everyone feels sorry for the Captain and Navigator who, presumably as a matter of course, will be court-martialled. Really, it is just one of those things that happen unexpectedly. But maybe the Navy will view it differently, with the embarrassment of it happening so far from home, and no nice British bases dotted about the place as there used to be.

It was one of those super days when everything turns into a nightmare at the end. It was lovely and warm and sunny, and we were anchored in a very secluded bay with sandstone rocks all around, which had been blown by the wind into "Swiss Cheese" shapes and were a lovely bright yellow, not the drab dirt-colour of Aqaba. Boats had gone ashore to the empty beaches with picnic parties, and it was rather like a pirate ship lying up in a secluded place before going to attack the enemy. The other ships were anchored further out to sea. It had been our first day in sight of land for a long time: really, since Aqaba, and we were having a day off after *Exercise Gonzo* with the Americans and a night exercise with the Omanis.

When we were weighing anchor, and about to leave, we suddenly hit a very bumpy patch – a bit like going up the track [to the cottage] at Clungunford in DOF [the car] – with about five bumps. Fortunately, the ship's hull was not holed. All the services are working . . . and no-one has been injured, and we have plenty of food and fuel in the supply ships: though quite how we are going to re-supply ourselves is more tricky. Presumably we will anchor a little distance from each other and the helicopter will bring the hose across (and the stores) . . . .

Having been initially elated by the news that we were scuppered I now feel more subdued by the thought of what will happen to the Captain and the Navigator. If we do refit out here we shall still come home on 26 February but if we are towed into Portsmouth we shall probably be back at the end of January. If they cut their losses and fly us home: who knows? But I think it most unlikely, because of the expense. I shall certainly not be able to look Gordon in the eye for a while.* I will write again soon.

* Gordon Hayes, a Clungunford friend who served in the Royal Navy during the second World War.

*To Christine*                                     HMS GLAMORGAN, *28 November 1981*

What news of the ship? Having fixed the propellers to allow us to chug around, we thought that C-in-C would allow us to stay out here, but I suppose they could not risk any further damage which would make us immobile and so ordered us home this morning. The chopping off of a piece of the propeller is taking longer than normal to achieve but I hope that we can still stick to our 21 December arrival date . . . .

It was vital that we stayed on station on an operational task, and the result of the grounding was that Britain could not maintain her stated presence of two warships in the Gulf. Even the P.M. will have been told about *Glamorgan* now. We are very much the naughty school-boy who has been sent home because he has misbehaved.

However, the poor Captain and Navigator apart, it really was a most excellent piece of damage. Without inconveniencing the life of anyone on board it has put paid to any more stupid exercising and has chopped two months off our deployment . . . I only wish it could have been [put down to] a recalcitrant stoker who we wanted to get rid of rather than the Captain, whose ship is his pride and joy, and who has given thirty-five years of faithful and unblemished service to the Navy . . . .

I'm thinking of you lots, Christine, and now more than ever. From now on it is a day nearer home every day. Here we are, in the bright blue sky, the strong sunshine, and the deeply brilliant blue sea, with the granite, rugged hills of Muscat jaggedly tumbling into the sea beside us. Little squat biblical-type houses are clustered on the only flat parts of sandy beach near the shore. And out in the bay, vast, empty oil tankers lie at anchor, so very unstable with no cargo, and their propellers sticking out of the water.

Yet in a month it will be back to dear Shropshire, with the sheep and trees and little lanes and the robins to feed. How delightful! These vast barren areas of sun-scorched land out here don't hold much attraction for me, although it is quite an experience to see them. I'd much rather be in the snow at Clungunford with Father Christmas climbing up and down our old chimney, and the Christmas decorations up. It's so exciting.

When we get back to Portsmouth I doubt that our entry will be greeted with much enthusiasm in the way that a band played and Flag Officer Portsmouth waved to us in his boat when we left. It will be a bit like Wilfred Owen:

> "A few, too few for guns or bells
> Will creep back to still village wells
> Up half-known roads"

(I've probably misquoted).*

– Except I shall probably toast Bandar Jissah Bay when we get back to Clungunford!

---

* David's ability to quote poetry from memory was a little astray here. See "The Send-Off": the last verse about the soldiers who return:
> Shall they return to beatings of great bells
> In wild train-loads?
> A few, a few, too few for drums and yells,
> May creep back, silent, to village wells,
> Up half-known roads.

*To H and E*                                          HMS GLAMORGAN,
                                                    *29 November 1981*

Thank you very much for your letters and Christmas present
which arrived the same day. It *would* have been marvellous to
see you in India [i.e. Karachi] in late January as our dates
would have coincided. However, we have since come to grief
at a very Kipling-type place in Muscat called Bandar Jissah
Bay where we found an unexpected rock and have written off
both propellers. We are now on our way back to Portsmouth
sounding very much like a washing machine as we churn
through the water, and the net result is that I'll see you for
Christmas! At least *Glamorgan* managed a bit further than *Fife*.

I shall have a week's leave from 23-30 December, so I expect
Christine and I will be coming north to see you, probably after
Christmas, if that sounds OK? The last time we saw you was
at Clungunford last Christmas wasn't it? We shall look forward
very much to seeing you again anyway.

You asked about . . . the cottage in your last letter . . . the
cottage has given us so much happiness and but for you it
would have gone to someone else.

Still savouring the last few days of sunshine just off Saudi
Arabia, but in fact even here it is starting to get a bit chilly. I
am quite looking forward to the Red Sea again to hot it up.
When we came through it was 120 degrees on deck in the sun
and 171 degrees between the boiler boxes.

See you in December.


*To Christine*                    HMS GLAMORGAN, *29 November 1981*

Now that our debts are all paid off I have begun to start
considering about the extension for the cottage. I have enclosed
a sketch, which is on the idea of a rounded end, with the
thatching radiating down from the gable end . . . . The advantage of it is that you don't have an end wall, so that if you
can't find the stone or can't manage timber framing this could
be the answer: building in brick with cement rendering and
white paint . . . . If we build the timber-framed barn on the
other end of the cottage as a barn or a garage we (a) avoid the

need to find some central beams for the joists for the upstairs ceiling (b) don't have to conform to building instructions because it won't be lived in . . . .

I have come to thinking of building in the modern way for the kitchen . . . because I feel it is starting to "drag on" . . . . The complications of trying to build [by ourselves] seem too enormous when we only have weekends, have no stone, no means of lifting or fixing together the beams, and not much chance of planning permission. The "rounded end" extension would not look too out of place; outside it would only be up to 7 feet high . . . .

Once I get back to UK I shall start looking to see how large showers, bogs, cookers and sinks actually are for fitting into the kitchen. I don't think we will really need very much space: it will certainly be three times the size of a minesweeper/ submarine galley!

Do you think this is a good idea or not? I know I have a completely opposite idea every week, so it is a bit hard to follow. But I am most enthusiastic about this idea – for this week, anyway!

Thinking of you lots and lots Christine.


*To Nigel Billington*                HMS GLAMORGAN, *12 December 1981*
                                                    *Mediterranean*


Happy Christmas! We are on our way back from the Persian Gulf after a *very* short patrol: 6,000 miles for a banyan! As soon as we arrived there we pranged a rock and wrote off both propellers, so we turned round and came back (nine weeks at sea to do what Concorde does in about three hours).

Thanks for all your letters and your kind card in April. I'm sorry I haven't written before . . . . I hope for your next appointment that you get what you want. I suppose, unlike the rest of us, you will avoid being a battery hen behind a typewriter by going to submarines. I told Nick you were volunteering and he went green with envy. Quite honestly, I should think they will retain him on the staff of the Chilean navy where he's gone with *Norfolk* to sell her off. He'd probably be a dab hand at torture!

Anyway, have a very happy Christmas, and I'll see you around sometime.

*To Christine*                    HMS GLAMORGAN, *21 February 1982*

At the moment I'm having to write very slowly because the ship is heaving about so much. We are in the area to the west of the Shetlands and the weather has been fairly ghastly all the way up from Portsmouth. Sitting up in my cabin just now I could hear the spray from the bow-waves breaking on the cabin roof, so you can imagine what it's like. All flying has now been cancelled through the strong winds (although the sky is lovely and bright) and we have been trying all day to fuel alongside our tanker. It was scheduled to be from 7 a.m. to 7.30, but at 1 p.m. we gave up, having tried all possible methods, because the ships were rolling around so much, with the sea pouring over the tanker's deck each time she heeled over. We are now heading for Hoy Sound in the Orkneys to find some shelter, where we should arrive at about 9 p.m. tonight.

I am now working Watches in the Ops Room (dreadful place) among all the fish-heads as "duty Staff Officer". None of us are really sure what we do, but it involves reading signals, all in Code: in figures and numbers and gobble-dy-gook, and trying to work out what they mean from recognising the odd word here and there: just like my medieval Spanish at University, really.

I have now heard that I will definitely be appointed to Chatham on Flag Officer Medway's staff to relieve Mike Rowlands (who gave us the nice flowery tea set) [as a wedding present] on 18 May. Plenty of time to finish off the sitting room at the cottage. I am very relieved that the job has nothing to do with *Pembroke*. I am really looking forward to this job very much: 18 months of RDP (run down period).

Unfortunately we have heard the news that the Captain and Navigator are going to be court-martialled, probably on 15 and 19 April. The charges are all very petty . . . and it makes me very angry that the Captain has not had any backing from the Commander-in-Chief who will in fact be on board when we become the Flagship for *Springtrain* in March-April. That will not be a pleasant time (as the decision went to him personally whether or not to proceed) . . . . Presumably, . . . [the Captain] will not be appointed as an ADC to the Queen, which is the normal consolation prize for Captains who don't make it to Admiral, which will be vindictive after his 35 years' service . . . .*

You have put me in a dilemma for the weekend of 13-14 March, as of course I would love to see you then but don't particularly want to hang around in Portsmouth. I think, if you don't mind too much, that I will go to the cottage then, as there is a good chance that I will be able to take the Monday off as well . . . .

[Christine managed to change her programme and they were able to spend the weekend together in their cottage: their last together.]

* On returning from the South Atlantic Captain Barrow was appointed ADC to the Queen.

*To H and E*                    HMS GLAMORGAN, *17 March 1982*

I didn't realise that you would be back from Burma so soon. Your stories of smugglers, bandits, boats at dawn and trains being blown up were quite amazing . . . . I am looking forward to hearing all your accounts when we see you next. Your journeys into areas barred to foreigners . . . make our visits to ports which have to have diplomatic clearance seem very tame.

Since Christmas we have been exercising to the west of the Shetlands, where it has been very stormy. We were with *Invincible*, and it was the first time I have operated in a group with carrier-borne aircraft. They were extremely good and could intercept all the raids coming in so that we didn't have the nail-biting finish of relying on our missiles!

Then we visited Antwerp, where I went on a trip to Ypres and Bruges. The numbers of war graves around Ypres is phenomenal. Just driving down the main road there are three or four signposts at each crossroads; and of course the Menin Gate is impressive and awesome. Bruges is a marvellous medieval town, in parts looking exactly the same as when it was painted by artists about 1600.

Now we have returned to our exercises and are off to Gibraltar with another twenty-three RN warships for *Exercise Springtrain*. I hope there will be room for us all in Gib! We are lucky enough to have the best berth as Commander-in-Chief Fleet is using us as his flagship. There are *so many* dinners and lunch parties during that time – it will all be very hectic and tense: even more so because at C-in-C's personal wish, Captain Barrow (his senior Captain) is going to be court-martialled in April for very niggling charges to do with our anchoring at Bandar Jissah Bay . . . . It is all very infuriating and shows that the C-in-C hasn't got the gumf to back Captain Barrow up, and do away with all the months of worry for him and the inevitable kick in the teeth, after his thirty-five years of unblemished and self-sacrificing service in the Navy – right at the end of his career. He leaves *Glamorgan*, which is his last job, in July . . . .

On a brighter subject, Christine has been playing plenty of sport and has now won her Army colours in hockey and table-tennis! She is finding it hard to fit in work at present . . . . My appointment to Chatham has now come through, as the Secretary to the Chief of Staff (who is a Captain) to Flag Officer, Medway. It all sounds very grand, but it is only pushing paper around. We will be moving into a married quarter . . . from 16 April and I start the new job on 18 May. It has all worked out very well and is quite incredible. You will have to come and visit us when you're next at Little Hampden . . . .

An amusing story from Clungunford is that the people who moved into the pretty "Old Rectory" next to the church, down our lane in October, have now moved out again. They made the mistake of riding through the Squire's Christmas shoot (without any apology) and were made instant social outcasts. It's very nice living there in the 19th Century.

I have finally remembered to enclose the photo which was taken at Kiel last year.

*To Christine*                    HMS GLAMORGAN, *24 March 1982*
                                              *At Gibraltar*

This should be my very last letter to you for a while. It's very exciting to think that it's only a few weeks until we move into our married quarter – a proper home for once! . . . .

We have now reached Gibraltar and all the nauseating performance [of ritual official visits] starts. We are, as you know, Commander-in-Chief's flagship; and if this wasn't enough the Captain slots his own dinner parties into every vacant mealtime. I shall be very glad to leave this ship with its petty problems . . . . Still, it's only twenty-five days to go.

It seems an awfully long time ago since I saw you, but in fact it is only ten days. Nothing much has happened since then at sea . . . exercises continue much as usual, although the weather is warmer down here . . . .

When I got to the station at Ludlow I found (which I should have known) that the first train on Sunday leaves at 3 p.m. I now know Ludlow quite well. There are two very good timber framed buildings which we haven't seen before – one behind the Church and one in an alley I didn't know existed, running parallel to and between Broad Street and Mill Street (part of the original medieval grid). There are a couple of little alleyways I hadn't seen before: one runs inside the old town wall . . . . I was very thankful for your nice packed lunch that day . . . .

# 5

## *To the South Atlantic, April-June 1982*

On Friday 2 April 1982, Argentinian armed forces took over the Falkland Islands. Immediately (as David wrote the same day) the ships assembled for *Springtrain* cancelled their exercise and departed for the South Atlantic. David and his own personal life suddenly became part of an international crisis.

David was later to emphasise that the order for their departure was issued without any prior consultation of Parliament. The debate which followed on Saturday 3 June was confused, with no rational analysis emerging. The opportunity for questioning the wisdom of initiating immediate naval action was lost. Hence, when *Hermes* and *Invincible* left three days later, amid enormous publicity, Britain was committed to a naval show of strength and the original cause of the Falklands occupation – which was the Conservative Government's policy of ending longstanding naval commitments in the South Atlantic – was allowed to fade from view.

The Commander of the Task Force, Rear Admiral Woodward, flew his flag in *Glamorgan* until they moved to the area of the Falklands, and then transferred to *Hermes* when the big ships joined them. The Admiral seems to have given the Task Force the impression that the mere threat of British sea power would be sufficient to make the Argentinians back down. The mood in the Task Force was light-hearted (as all those involved relate). It was a very welcome break from routine, and an opportunity to show that Britannia still rules the waves. However, the Gods of War scented blood. This time, Space Age technology would ensure that the bloodshed would be even more random and unrelated to human endeavour than in the carnage of the Great War.

Secretary of State Haig came and went. He was unable to make deals with parties who refused to negotiate except upon *their own* terms. And so the show of strength must introduce the use of force. The Argies must be taught a lesson. *Glamorgan* was ordered into close action against the main Argentinian forces at Stanley. This was on 1st May. To their amazement their enemy reacted with equal force. *Glamorgan* came under attack from modern aircraft armed with the most modern means of destruction. It was just luck which saved them from immediate extinction.

Next day, a British submarine sank the vintage Argentinian cruiser *Belgrano*. This caused the greatest loss of life throughout the conflict. If this seemed a British success it was immediately cancelled out by the sinking of the British destroyer, *HMS Sheffield*.

For the very first time the British people grasped that they were at war: a war in which the enemy held as many military trumps as we did. The loss of *Sheffield* showed that British warships were not invulnerable.

David had realised already that military force offered no long-term solution, but appalled by the loss of lives and the sinking of a fine destroyer he began to work out the whole question of what they were supposed to be doing. The mood in the Task Force was now sombre. Their ships, that they had supposed to be so well-designed and equipped, now appeared to offer no sure defence. The enemy, who they had been told were comic opera warriors, showed they were capable of sustained attack. It was war, not just a demonstration.

David felt that his questioning of the way force was being used was a quirk of his own until he received letters from his parents and from his brother Jonathan which revealed that back at home people he loved were thinking along the same lines. His letters became increasingly critical and searching. He poured out his thoughts to Christine and also to his friends, Gordon and Marion. He also discussed his viewpoint with his brother officers. Some of them agreed with him, while others, who differed, respected his ideas. David would have said, as did W. B. Yeats:

Those that I fight I do not hate.*

*Glamorgan* was in almost continuous action, including the raid upon Pebble Island which attracted such attention in the press. David observed that his friends were showing signs of strain. He seems to have managed to survive relatively un-

---

* "An Irish Airman Foresees his Death" (already quoted by Dave).

scathed because his secret life since boyhood in company with the fighters of the Great War had conditioned him to confront death as part of reality. After a month of continuous action *Glamorgan* was ordered to leave the vicinity of the Falklands and proceed to the "back area" where a rendezvous had been marked out for the supply ships and the reinforcements. For a welcome period of eight days *Glamorgan* was given the job of marshalling the merchant ships and organising their disposal. However, the war on land was moving towards its climax. The advance by the troops had been interrupted for the visit to Britain by the Pope and by the American President. It was right that hostilities should not be escalated while Pope John Paul was on his mission of peace, but it was inexcusable that everything had to stop while Reagan disported himself with the Queen. With him out of the way, the battle recommenced.

Once again *Glamorgan* was ordered close inshore for nightly bombardments in support of the British land forces advancing on Port Stanley. To avoid Argentinian air attack, the night's shelling would cease at 6 a.m. when the ship would make for the open sea. On the night 11-12 June, *Glamorgan* carried out yet another bombardment and stood close inshore – not much more than a quarter of a mile from land. At 6 a.m. as usual the guns stopped firing and they stood out to sea. The Argentinians had mounted an Exocet missile on a truck and chose this moment to fire. The missile was seen to approach: the ship fired one of its own anti-missile missiles in reply, but it failed to explode the oncoming Exocet, deflecting it only, so that instead of hitting *Glamorgan* just above the waterline – which would have sunk the ship – the missile hit the Flight Deck before exploding downwards into the galley. David, and the men on the Flight Deck were killed instantly. Those in the galley were mortally wounded. Helicopters arrived from *Invincible* to transport them to the carrier with its better operating facilities. But of those who were wounded, only one survived.

*Glamorgan* moved out into the ocean, and the same evening a burial service was held for the thirteen who had lost their lives. In traditional navy fashion, in shrouds inscribed with messages from their friends, and draped with the White Ensign, they were laid on the poop deck while the ship's company assembled on the Flight Deck above. After a short service, one by one they were committed to the deep.

Two days later the Argentinian commander on the Falklands surrendered his forces to the British.


*To H and E*                              HMS GLAMORGAN, *2 April 1982*

Thank you for your long letter. This is just a quick one to say that today we have heard the news that we are off to the Falkland Islands to bash the Argentinians. This is great fun, and very much like Maggie Thatcher to stick up for our few remaining colonies with a show of force! A great Fleet is assembling, both our carriers, *Hermes* and *Invincible*, the two County Class destroyers, *Antrim* and ourselves, three Type 42 destroyers, three Type 21 frigates (both classes are very modern) a nuclear submarine, *Superb* (sshh)* and *Brilliant*, *Exeter*, and two store ships: with *Endurance*, sixteen ships down there.

At the moment we have just cancelled the exercise. We are transferring stores, and are just about to set off south from the Gibraltar exercise area. We are due to call in at Ascension Island and pass by St Helena: very much a 1914 affair, with the Royal Navy going off to defend her colonies (or should I be thinking of Suez?). The Americans, this time, seem to be on our side, but we have only heard "buzzes", not having had newspapers for some time. It is anyway all very exciting.

Unfortunately, it means I shall miss moving into our cosy married quarters for another couple of months, and Easter leave goes by the board. But this is much more fun. Surprisingly, the Argentinians have quite a good navy: a carrier with strike aircraft (like the old *Ark Royal*) and three Type 42 destroyers. If *Superb* sinks the carrier we will take care of the rest.

Of course, the whole thing may blow over in a week, but the thrill of some real confrontation away from the nuclear bombs of the northern world in a "colonial war" is quite exciting compared to the usual dull routine of exercises and paper-

* David appears to have swallowed the same story as the rest of us. *Superb* never went to the South Atlantic. This seems to have been officially-inspired disinformation.

work (although these will still continue: we shall probably "work up" as we go south).

The Captain is of course delighted: he may be able to finish his career in a blaze of glory . . . . All for now, as this must be posted before the ships separate and we head south for the penguins.

*To Christine*                        HMS GLAMORGAN, *2 April 1982*

Although my last letter to you *should* have been the last, this one – and probably one or two more – may be all that you hear of me for a while. We are off to the Falkland Islands as you have probably heard on the news to do a bit of Wog-Bashing! There's a terrific force of ships assembling . . . sixteen British warships steaming south across the Atlantic at a great rate of knots – terrific!

It reminds me that in the Great War when Commodore Craddock was sunk with his force of three ships at Coronel by the Germans (who had a similar sized but better armed force) Britain sent absolutely everything down to the Falklands and gave the Germans a real pounding. I think the Admiralty has learnt its lesson . . . . On the way down to the Falklands we are stopping at Ascension Island, another British colony, and passing St Helena (yet another). This really is like the days of 1914 and great fun.

Unfortunately, of course, this means that Easter leave and everything goes for a burton, and I'm truly sorry about that, but it can't really be helped. Unless you hear anything on the radio or in newspapers to say that we are coming back you will have to work on the assumption that I probably won't be back until July. One month there and back, and two months on patrol . . . . As soon as I have news of our return I will let you know, but the last post is likely to be from Ascension Island and then I'm not sure whether telegrams work from down under . . . .

*To Mike Rowlands*                         HMS GLAMORGAN,
           *(somewhere outside England) [received, 15 April 1982]*

My profound apologies on behalf of the Argentinians! I
know how much you must be itching to get to Yeovilton, and
I too would much rather be in Chatham than here.

It is anybody's guess as to when we get back, and I suppose
the appointer will pick up the pieces from there. I shouldn't
think there is much joy to be wrought from him at the
moment . . . .

If it is any consolation, I don't expect you to give me much
of a handover after all this: a few jotted notes left on the desk
as you disappear at a great rate of knots will be enough.

See you when I see you.


*To H and E*          HMS GLAMORGAN, *No date [received 16 April]*

Just a quick note to say that we are all fine and having fun
playing our war games. One advantage of the Falklands is that
you have to go through the tropics first, so we are all getting
a good sun tan.

I am sure you are quite sick of hearing about the Falklands
by now on the TV. We are kept up to date very well by the
BBC World Service, and the conversation on board is always
about the latest "buzz": the state of the negotiations, the plans
for the ship, the latest intelligence about the Argentinians –
and how each person thinks we should fight the war.

We are now resplendent in our war-paint (though not,
unfortunately, dazzle-paint),* but these days of course it is all
space-age stuff and not so much like the films where they took
off their white cap-covers on the bridge before a battle and
had duffle-coats and cocoa (although both would be very
welcome where we are going).†

My position is down on the Flight Deck, so I am lucky in
having the warmest clothing issued of anyone on board. At the

* A reference to camouflage techniques in the First World War?
† We thought this was a hint that *Glamorgan* would be sent to South
  Georgia.

moment, of course, it is delicious down there; a hot sun, with a cooling breeze blowing over the deck.

It looks like anybody's guess as to how long this is all going to last, but in any case I suppose there will now be a standing naval patrol down there. So I hope I will see you at Christmas! There is probably going to be a gap in the mail from now (which is nice from the Secretarial side) for some time, but I shall write again later with some more news.


*To Christine*                    HMS GLAMORGAN, *7 April 1982*


This is, in fact, the last letter that I will be sending you for a while until Chile starts sending our mail back for us. But then, of course, it will be censored and even though only by the padre, doctor or dentist [they are] not people who I want to read my personal thoughts to you. I love you very much indeed and hope that you are not worrying about it all. It is much easier for me, here, because it is really very exciting, but I know how I would feel if you were away. Rest assured, that even if the worst happens [they were sunk] I am in one of the best places in the ship. I shall be in the hangar or on the Flight Deck all the time. The hangar is the best protected place, with thick double doors, and the life rafts are right next to us. We have extra water and are stocking up with chocolate and biscuits which we'll carry in our gas mask bags. If it hasn't all been solved by the time we get down there we shall be sleeping on camp beds in the hangar where it is only a five seconds dash to the open. We wear very thick clothing all the time and have plastic suits which cover us completely (like a big bag) for jumping into the water. The life rafts are also very good with stocks of water, radios, etc. I am only telling you this so that you know we are in the best position possible to survive, on the Flight Deck. I am sure it won't come to it anyway. The Argentinians must be frightened to see such a large fleet coming towards them.

If it does come to a war there won't be much of a naval battle. Our submarines can take out their aircraft carrier and Type 42s [destroyers] (built in Barrow!) and we can take care of the rest. All our weapons are designed for their generation of forces. I doubt if the Argentinians will want to risk sending their ships out. If they are sunk, they will have nothing to stop us bombarding Buenos Aires. —— even said "Drop a big white job (Polaris) on them". Thank goodness he's not in command.

The main threat is from air attack, and all our ships are air defence ships: with, of course, the Sea Harriers, which are very good. We have Seaslug and Seadart long-range anti-aircraft missiles, and Seacats and guns for close range. And we have got plenty of them!

The most amusing thing is that it will be difficult to find the Falkland islanders [amidst all the combatants]. With only 1,800 of them, there are, I suppose, 15,000 RN personnel, 4,000 army – 4,000 Argentinian army, and say 3,000 Argentinian navy: outnumbering the islanders by about twelve to one!

The good thing about it is that there is stacks of time left for some sort of compromise. Which I am sure will happen. Things seem to be happening slowly but surely on that front. More and more allies for us (including the French!)* a base in Chile,† mediation by the USA etc. We get all our information from the World Service of the BBC (just like *Yes Minister*) although our own signals tell us what our own forces are doing, which is circulated by "buzz". As you can imagine, the whole ship is throbbing with buzzes. Even the Navigator has stopped talking about his rock, thank goodness: bye-bye court martial.‡ All the talk is about the latest developments; how each person thinks we should fight the war; the ups and downs, as the situation unfolds; cheering for the Marines when we heard that they had shot a corvette with their Charlie-G.§ The sailors are all very amusing with their jokes about it all.

The advent of this whole new lifestyle is really quite strange.

* Makers of the Exocet which killed David.
† Why this myth about Chilean support (see also above)? Was there some indication at this stage that Chile would give facilities, or was this just part of the propaganda war which MOD and the BBC waged: to very little effect?
‡ After the South Atlantic operation the directions for the court martial of the Captain and Navigator were quashed: though not before they had expended money on fees for Barristers, etc.
§ When the Argentinians landed in South Georgia the tiny Marine garrison succeeded in disabling a ship by using a weapon intended against aircraft.

Normal days and weeks are put into abeyance. Routine paperwork becomes unnecessary. The ship's programme becomes non-existent. We're here, until something else happens. There is no set pattern or framework for it all. The comforts of life, and the goodies – leave, pay, fun time in foreign ports – all become irrelevant. We are now actually doing something which we have always thought about as likely as Men on Mars!

*To Christine*                    HMS GLAMORGAN, *10 April 1982*

You may have been wondering whether or not to move into the Married Quarter, but I should think you have gone ahead anyway. My guess is that I won't be back for some time – probably September – and then, of course, appointments, turnovers etc. have to be re-arranged so it may be as late as October before I get to Chatham. It all depends on whether a settlement can be reached, but even then we may be left to patrol the area . . . .

You must be sick of hearing and reading about the Falklands by now. BBC World Service news bulletins are still three-quarters composed of it, so the domestic services must be full of it . . . . We maintain a glue-like interest in the news and are all clustered round the radio when it is broadcast. Conversation is always about the latest "buzz", the state of the negotiations, the plans for the ship, and the latest intelligence about the Argentinians. As we get nearer we have lost the euphoria – accompanied by depression – and are getting more determined that we must do our job well to defeat the Argentinians and survive. Reality is dawning rapidly.

At times the situation seems so absolutely silly: here we are, in 1982, fighting a colonial war on the other side of the world: 28,000 men going to fight over a fairly dreadful piece of land inhabited by 1,800 people. After it is all over and millions of pounds have been expended they will be left in peace (having had their homes destroyed by shelling) and the 28,000 men will then go away again. Moreover, one side [Britain] has supplied the other with its weapons so that the war can be started in the first place – and both sides end up impoverished.

The *ideal* is most praiseworthy: the wishes of a tiny people being supported by the might of a large industrialised state. Everything else is quite ludicrous. It has given us some time in the sun, and a break from the horrid, rough weather up by the Shetlands – just in time for the horrid weather of the Falklands! It is interesting, anyway, preparing to go to war: even if, hopefully, everyone sees sense before long.

It is certainly something I have often thought about before now; and to a certain extent a boy's upbringing is centred on warlike activities and war stories. If we can have a few shots over the bow that will be quite enough, and honour will be satisfied. I personally do not want to kill any Argentinians, or anybody else. However, I have always felt that it is something one is bound to do at some stage. With a grandfather in France, 1915-18, his brother going on to the Archangel campaign in Russia and winning an MC, great-grandfather McKenzie in the Sudan, Elisabeth's brother Peter in the RAF [killed in the Western Desert], Hugh in Burma: Tinkers and relations have covered quite a few wars in the last hundred years! I shall be happy if we call it a day after this one.

It is a very unreal time. All the preparations for war are carried out, which one always thinks of as happening in war films only: but are actually happening now. It is almost like a gigantic spoof. Time is also unreal. The days pass at their usual speed, but it seems ages since we left Gibraltar – yet only two weeks ago. The longest time was when *Hermes* etc. were preparing to sail. It seemed weeks before they were ready, but in fact only a weekend: and amazing for Pompey dockyard! It must have been a fascinating sight to see all the preparations taking place, I wish I had been there. It must have been a bit like D-Day. We have also been hearing wonderful things about the speed of the dockyard since then also . . . . The most odd thing is not having a ship's programme and not having a calendar of "days left to do in *Glamorgan*", I am still holding the count-down at 15. The best thing, I suppose, for us both is to live day to day. Each day comes with its own small achievements and blessings, and there is contentment in living like that. Certainly there's no point in being depressed by looking at too big a chunk of the future.

David and Christine working on the cottage

*Glamorgan:* dawn on the flight deck (David in anti-flash gear on right)

*To Christine*                              HMS GLAMORGAN, *12 April 1982*

It's been a bit of a working Easter, here. It must be the first time I haven't been to church on Easter Day. We were flying all day, and now I look like I have spent all my life in the open air on the African Veldt. As we are now at Ascension Island (sshh) the stores are coming in at a steady rate by helicopter. I didn't know how well equipped Ascension was – it has a good runway which takes Nimrods and Hercules (sshh) and lots of radar, radio and oil tanks, plus a harbour – and of course still part of the British Empire. We have had our first newspapers and I didn't realise how much information was being let out. I notice that the Navy is upgrading everything. *Invincible* is called a Carrier, not a "through-deck cruiser". We are called "light cruisers" not "destroyers", etc. This is in fact thë correct terminology, and I'm glad they are using the proper terms at last.

The *Portsmouth News* was of course full of the send-off for *Hermes* and *Invincible*. Enormous photographs: flags waving, mothers weeping, etc. All good stuff. Now we have had the fun of it all, let's go home.

Things look much more hopeful for a successful conclusion by negotiations. The Argentinians have withdrawn their navy, sensibly; and the Falklanders must surely see that they won't get exactly what they want over this war. Either they have a huge battle and remain British for a few more years before the Argentinians try again when we haven't got a Navy left, or they accept a compromise. Once people in Britain see that inflation is going up because the pound is falling, and that they have to pay for a war or naval patrol in taxes, then they may get fed up with the Falklands anyway. Wars are always economic disaster for a country (apart from our 19th century colonial wars) so let us finish it while we are still at the flag-waving stage and enjoying it all. Honour would be satisfied if one of our submarines could just sink a small Argentinian ship (preferably without loss of life).

I received your letter of 6 April today. It must be totally depressing with everyone going around saying what a super thing this Argentinian war is and you telling them to shut up! The news now seems very encouraging, so that with any luck we should spend a couple of weeks in the tropics and then go home . . . . Programmes in the Navy change rapidly and the most reliable source of information is the Chief Cook in the main galley – honestly . . . . I have already had to write five thank you letters to people sending us good luck telegrams. If you had said to me that even in the middle of preparations for war I'd be writing thank you letters . . . . I suppose I would have believed you!

Life here is almost delicious. The sky and sea are very blue, it is marvellously warm, with a nice sea breeze to cool you down, and there is the lovely island to look at: magnificent volcanic peaks towering up to one enormous mountain with its head in the clouds. It really is the most perfect setting.

Mail should now be fairly quick and there are plenty of flights at the moment to and from UK. The trip back should be rather nice as well, except for the paperwork . . . . I don't think that I will get any leave now . . . . At least we will be together, anyway.

*To Christine*                    HMS GLAMORGAN, *14 April 1982*

I must admit it is a problem what to do about the Quarter. Your guess is as good as mine as to when we'll be back. I suspect that they will settle by the end of the week, but the *Sunday Mirror* had a rather good battle plan in it, in which we attack South Georgia with *Glamorgan* shown at the back (phew) out of range of their aircraft. In other words, we can bash them but they can't bash us: a good plan! That has made me feel more like a battle now! I don't know if you saw the *Sunday Mirror* for Easter Day, but it was a good plan and the kind Mirror-men sent it to us free. Very nice of them. Anyway, it will give our Admiral some ideas (he has been on board with his staff for the past fortnight). I chuckled when I read in the paper – cuttings that had been sent to us – that the Admiral would already have formulated his ideas for an attack, based on the best naval intelligence. Our intelligence consists of the "Schoolie", who knew where the Falklands were because he had an Atlas, and *Jane's Fighting Ships* to tell us what the Argentinians had in their navy. As for the plan of attack, nobody knew what to do. Fighting submarines and ships at sea is OK for Admirals; but they never give a thought about how to attack an island. Now we have got some newspapers it has given the staff some ideas: most likely they will go for the *Mirror* plan. And we've got the charts of the Falkland Islands today, so we know where to go. Intelligence has also done a good job, and from knowing nothing about the Argentinians a fortnight ago we now know quite a lot. But I wonder if the newspaper-men know how invaluable they have been.

As for the ship, we have been drifting about off Ascension for the past few days. We are now going up to join the *Hermes* group where the staff will go, and I can return to my cabin from the grot in which I have been sleeping. Mind you, it has its advantages: I don't think I have seen a porny mag since I was in the *Hermes* grot.

We have dispensed with the thought of censorship of mail now. The press aboard *Hermes* and *Invincible* seem to give everything away. Jolly clever of them to find so much to write about every day and get it sent back to England, photos and all every day, even when right out at sea with no mail drops.

*To Christine*                                    HMS GLAMORGAN, *16 April 1982*
                                                              *At Ascension Island*

Well, here we are back at Ascension Island again. It is becoming quite a home to us, and it was a very welcoming sight when we saw it on the horizon this morning. It is a very distinguished-looking island indeed. We had been going north to meet up with the *Hermes* heavy mob, and actually saw *Hermes* for the first time this morning. She is absolutely crammed with Sea King (large) helicopters and Harriers, and there must be quite a scrum below decks: two thousand people on board. We were steaming along with her this morning and her Harriers were flying overhead, giving all the ships in the group some aircraft "targets" to lock on to. The Harriers really are magnificent aircraft, and it makes us all feel a lot safer to have them in our group.

The ships which we were with at Ascension have now all departed to destinations unknown:* so having the staff on

* *Antrim*, *Glamorgan's* sister ship departed for South Georgia with other vessels.

board was worthwhile. The Captain said over the broadcast yesterday that he knew we must all be disappointed in not going, but never mind, our time would come .... Certainly, we much prefer being in the main carrier group which has air cover and which will be kept at arm's length from the enemy .... Anyway, we have got to stay at Ascension for a few more days yet ....

The news on the war front is more and more exciting. The Argentinian Fleet putting to sea, so we might get a chance to sink them (although I doubt that they'll venture outside Argentinian coastal waters). Twenty RAF ground attack Harriers coming on the next container ship (as opposed to ours, which are interceptors). More troops coming in the *Uganda*. And tons of ships coming in a month's time, including *Illustrious* (our *third* aircraft carrier) which hasn't even done the Portland work-up yet.* And the French are going to provide air-launched Exocet missiles (*the* missile we are scared of from the Argentinians: twenty miles range, sea-skimming, and almost invulnerable) for our helicopters to carry: in addition to "Sea-Skuas" for our Lynx helicopters. This wasn't due to enter service until 1985, and is even better than Exocet. Ho ho ho: spend lots of government money, depress the pound, put up inflation: what fun! Man is the most extraordinary animal.

I cannot believe that the Argentinians will want to fight with all this lot coming against them. Already they look to be in danger of spending all their foreign currency reserves and losing all ability to obtain loans in the western world. Surely they must give in soon: hopefully, over the weekend, and then we can all go home.

I suppose you must be pretty fed up of hearing about the Falklands, but it is quite exciting being at a particular spot where all the front pages of the newspapers are focussing on. Something that I will never experience again. I was looking at *Hermes* today, where the journalists are, thinking that in the British press just *here* is where the Number One story in the world is coming from. I'm sure you would feel just as excited about it all if you were here. It is also special because it is something that you can't just "get in on the act" in, and something that we are all caught up in: and can't get out of.

* This was yet another buzz without any foundation.

Something where you see the forces of Government and State dictating to the individual to do something he doesn't want to do at all. It's quite fascinating.

We are now fully prepared for "war". My cabin is secured for action. It looks very tidy. And we all have our dog tags – Geneva Convention ID Cards, and first field dressings. Giving them out yesterday was a sobering thought for most people: reminding them that the "From the Cradle to the Grave" Service was now catering for situations where they could be blown to bits, interrogated, or laid out on a slab. Not the sort of things one wants to be reminded of! (And I wouldn't mention them in this letter if I thought that there was the remotest chance of any of them happening). Being at war doesn't stop the Captain from dishing out little jobs in abundance now the Admiral has gone: even to amending the Wardroom families guide (which I had to do "immediately" over the lunch hour between action stations and being on the Flight Deck) .... I am *definitely* leaving the Navy in the next round of redundancies if I can. Doing warlike things is quite fun, but peacetime activities are dreadful.

Everything is now painted in wartime colours and looks very dashing. The helicopter is now dark blue, with black lettering and roundels of red and light blue. The Harriers are similarly dark grey. On the Flight Deck you can now do "wartime" things. I landed a Sea King helicopter on deck the other day; once in daylight, and once at night. You are not supposed to, because they are much too big; but it was great fun and much more convenient for people getting in and out, than slowly winching them up. I want to land a Harrier on deck next! I am sure it would fit OK.

That's all from "War Special" for the moment .... I suppose you will stay in barracks for the moment, will you? You'd find it pretty horrid coming home to an empty quarter every night. I hope everything else is going OK .... This news that *Glamorgan* is right at the back of it all should put your mind at rest and allow you to concentrate on the important things of life, like tennis. Hope you've won a few more trophies for Owl and Penguin to sit in by the time I get back. All my love comes to you with this letter ....

*To Christine*          HMS GLAMORGAN, *17 April 1982: 10 p.m.*
*At Ascension Island*

This is it: the buzz has come that we are being ordered south, in command of a force of nine ships. *Hermes* and *Invincible* are remaining at Ascension to wait for their aviation fuel. The Captain/Commander won't tell us where we are going, or even that we are going, but will probably come up on the broadcast tomorrow, saying that we have been lucky enough to be selected to go south – and next mail will be in three months' time! I have dashed up to write this letter to you to let you know: a helicopter will take it ashore tomorrow morning, so it should get to you. It's very much "Like wrongs hushed-up, they went".* In the middle of the night, without even being told we're going.

Let us hope that by the time you read this the Argies will have settled, or that we have gone to South Georgia – who knows? There are still 2,000 miles between us and them . . . .

It is unfortunate that we are leaving the *Hermes* group as the press won't now be able to report back where *Glamorgan* is, so I doubt you'll see any mention of us. I don't even know where the other ships are which left previously. Let us just hope that everyone stays cool . . . .

Well, here we are: Ascension Island at night, all fully stored, fully fuelled: the middle of the night in the balmy tropics, waiting for orders. Exciting little plastic shapes in the Ops Room at Northwood. All eager to push them forward. We go forward, and the whole Navy follows. Only eight anti-submarine frigates are going to be left to guard Britain.

Anyway, lots of love for now. Next letter follows in two months' time: less, if the Argies and Maggie see sense.

* Wilfred Owen: *The Send-Off:*
  So secretly, like wrongs hushed-up they went. They were not ours:
  We never heard to which front these were sent.

*To Christine*          HMS GLAMORGAN, *18 April 1982*

Just a quick note, as there may be a helicopter to take this ashore. We are now going to the Falklands with the two carriers and *Fearless*, so fortunately we are still with the heavy mob.

We had some excitement this morning, with a Russian submarine at Ascension. Its periscope was seen by one of the tankers (!) and we have been playing cat and mouse with it since. Never mind, so long as we take the tankers with us we should be able to ward off the Argentinian submarines.

*To Christine*                              HMS GLAMORGAN, *3 May 1982*
                                                           *At the Falklands*

Although the mail doesn't go off that often now I am hopeful that this will reach you before too long via one of our returning stores ships. I am sorry that there's been a long gap in letters but . . . we are all fine out here. The weather is not as bad as they make out. Just like England in fact. Yesterday was a lovely sunny day with a very calm sea. The wildlife out here is super, and so much of it! Some beautiful albatrosses have been following the ship with their enormous wings . . . . Also, some lovely white doves; brown, well-fed looking birds (a bit like our Penguin); geese with long necks and plump black and white bodies. They all fly round regularly when we are close to land. It's very nice looking at them all on the Flight Deck when we are at action stations (we thought we should take some bread up to feed them, as the war rages around). The Falklands themselves look a bit like the Shetlands: it all looks very peaceful and still, in there.

The war has gone fine so far. The stories from South Georgia are quite amusing. When the British troops (79) advanced into the main square they found the Argentinians sitting round the edge, smoking, weapons piled in the middle, all ready to give in against superior odds. The sea battles have produced some good results as well: one cruiser, one submarine, and two patrol craft lost by the Argentinians. The Harriers are proving very good indeed; stopping Argentine aircraft at seventy miles away.

The war for *Glamorgan* started on 1 May (a date I won't forget), as the main force moved towards the Falklands we went on ahead to do some shelling of the airport . . . . The

Royal Marines on the signal deck . . . strapped to the Oerlikon guns, very exposed, shouted to the Mirages as they went past "Come here you buggers, let me get at you". The Argentinians claimed us as damaged, but this was only because we engaged our gas turbines with a will, and sent up an enormous plume of smoke. They actually didn't touch us. The outcome of it all was that we are not going to do shelling again in daylight, but only at night, when their aeroplanes can't fly for various navigational reasons. It is quite safe then. They only have howitzers which can't shoot us moving around . . . .

I hope things haven't been too bad for you at home. It must be most frustrating when you hear the news of all this instantly, but don't get a letter to say how we are for weeks. Anyway, no news is good news. It is amazing though how quickly these events are broadcast. We started our barrage at 7.15 p.m. and fell out from action stations at 9.30 p.m.* By 10.00 p.m. it was in the BBC World Service news, having gone via Argentinian fighter pilots to Argentina, and then to the press, and then to London and the BBC. And we heard about the torpedoing of the Argentinian cruiser on the radio half an hour before the signal came from MOD confirming it . . . .

Don't worry about us here. We are all in very good spirits, laughing and joking. The sailors' humour remains very funny in these circumstances. I often think of you, and think you would find a lot of their stories amusing (the more distant the time the event took place, the more elaborate the details become).

We should receive some mail today, so I will probably get tons of your letters, but the last one I had from you was dated 6 April, so probably quite a lot has happened to you since then. Have you got your new car yet? If you bought it on 1 May I hope it came fitted with Sidewinder missiles. After all, you never know what you might come upon these days. I hope Maggie will have had enough of her war soon and then we can all go home and become schoolteachers, vicars and ban the bomb enthusiasts.

* These timings are GMT, not local time, which was hours earlier.


*To Christine*                     HMS GLAMORGAN, *5/6 May 1982*


[After *HMS Sheffield* was sunk on 4 May, every member of *Glamorgan's* ship's company was allowed to send a cable home by "Modmail Familygram" to next of kin to reassure them. David chose to send Christine a poem by W. B. Yeats: or rather, part of a poem, as he was limited in the number of words he could send. The poem follows, with the lines he actually sent in italics.]

> *Had I the heavens' embroidered cloths,*
> Enwrought with golden and silver light,
> *The blue and the dim and the dark cloths*
> *Of night and light and the half-light;*
> *I would spread the cloths under your feet:*
> But I, being poor, have only my dreams;
> I have spread my dreams under your feet;
> Tread softly because you tread on my dreams.

*To Julian Salmon*                    HMS GLAMORGAN, *6 May 1982*

How *very* nice to hear from you. I really was quite amazed when I opened your letter, it is so long since we last saw each other . . . . I think it was when you were about to go to Keele University that I wrote to you last, wasn't it? Since then I have remained, somewhat surprisingly, in the Navy. I married a girl called Christine two years ago . . . . Our permanent address is in Shropshire at 4 Church Row, Clungunford, if ever you want to write again . . . .

Thank you so much for writing, Julian, with your marvellous peaceful message. There is very little of that here, as you can imagine and it is very welcome. We live on an air of tension here, not sleeping but just dozing, ready with our gear, waiting for the action stations buzzer announcing another air raid. The picture that Nott and his cronies are giving is not true. The Argentinian air force has the latest attack aircraft and missiles, which we just do not have. We long for nights, when their aircraft cannot attack us, and at the moment we are rejoicing in a fog which is sheltering us. I wish the politicians would see sense and stop the war. What is happening here is barbaric and totally unnecessary. It is disgusting that two Christian and humane countries (one at least!) should resort to this, all for some petty reason.

Do you remember when we were studying Wilfred Owen at

Mill Hill? In his poem where he says "Oh death was never enemy of ours . . . . We whistled while he shaved us with his scythe", he ends up (I'm probably misquoting) "There'll come a day when men make war on death for lives – not men for flags".* This is what it is, a war for a flag . . . I think that Maggie Thatcher sees herself as a Churchill, and as for Nott . . . let him come and lie down on the deck with us while the air raids come in and the missiles go off. He would see what it is really like and soon change his tune.

I never would have thought that I would be writing to you in the middle of a war! Let us hope that it ends SOON . . . . You didn't mention what you were doing now . . . . I hope you are finding satisfaction in your life, anyway, and hopefully achieving fulfilment of what you want to do. We must meet in London when I return . . . . All my very best wishes and thoughts for you now.

* The last lines of "The Next War" are a little different:
  We laughed, knowing that better men would come,
  and greater wars; when each proud fighter brags
  He wars on Death – for Life; not men – for flags.


*To H and E*     HMS GLAMORGAN, *6 May 1982 [received 30 May]*

Thank you very much for your letters of 19 April which arrived today. This should return to you, courtesy of *British Esk* as she comes down with more fuel. It must be a worrying time for you at home with all this dreadful business going on. But we are all fine, and in good heart, and have not been touched. We cannot really believe it is happening and we all hope for peace: as I am sure do the Argentinian soldiers.

I only hope that pressure is brought to bear on the British Government by the UN, USA and EEC to stop the war. It is British action that is causing the actual fighting; the Argentinians merely return like with like . . . . I hope that the Government falls quickly on a vote of no-confidence or that they see sense and agree to a cease-fire. The other measures being taken – world pressure and economic sanctions – are quite enough for solving the dispute over a rock with a village population. It is just a question of which flag flies.

Thank you for the rest of the news especially about Little

Hampden . . . I suppose it is now almost twenty years since we first went to Hampden. I hope Mr Hill [the Rector] is still in good form . . . .

The weather down here is, surprisingly, quite good and the sea has been calmer than the usual English Channel and much calmer than off the Shetlands where we carry out our big exercises. We have also seen some lovely birds, and the area is teeming with wildlife. Albatrosses have often followed us with their huge wingspan, so slowly floating just above the surface of the water without a movement and turning by almost dipping one wing in the water. We have also seen some big owl-like birds and black and white small Canada geese/penguin birds. The sailors have all kept their Penguin chocolate biscuit wrappers and have popped them in among dials in the engine-room so that wherever you go Penguins are keeping an eye on you.

That's all for now. I'm sure you are keeping an eye out for Christine at this time. Let us hope that it is all over by the time you get this letter.

*To Christine*                    HMS GLAMORGAN, *8 May 1982*

I don't know when this letter will reach you. Yours of 23 April reached me today, which is only two weeks: quite quick, as the letters go by ship until Ascension, and then by air to Britain. This one should come to you courtesy of *British Esk*, which has come down to refuel us.

I'm very glad to hear about your new car, and I hope it's giving you lots of pleasure, only I hope you don't go too whizzy when I get back. I have been used to very slow speeds since the middle of February. I hope that staying in barracks isn't too wearisome either: more of that dreadful lampshade . . . . I'm also glad that Mrs Barrow has been in touch. She often has some up-to-date news, although it tends to be a bit "yo-ho" as supplied by Captain B. However, he does sometimes signal information to her (like when we are coming home, etc.) which is always useful to know. We are also allowed to send telegrams from *Glamorgan* every so often so don't get worried when they turn up. Also, if you are feeling fed up Hugh and

Elisabeth are always on the phone and will be writing to you. I'm sure if you wanted to get away from Chattenden barracks they would be very happy to have you to stay.

What of things down here? It is all pretty quiet, really: a couple of alarums and excursions, but nothing is really going on. We get a bit excited when we think rocks and clouds are enemy ships and aircraft, and the Harriers get a bit of a surprise when nothing is there! Since the *Sheffield*, the Task Force has moved away from the islands right to the edge of the exclusion zone, and often outside. We are out of range of enemy aircraft over here. It is 600 miles from their bases to get here, so on fuel alone they are not going to be bothered. They also can't operate at night, and yippee, the nights get longer every day [sic]. Also, the news out of *Sheffield* is comforting (one can hardly call it good) in that 90 per cent of the people on board survived an attack which it had previously been thought would do much more damage. The Argentinians only have two of those missiles left. They shot two at *Sheffield* and one missed.* And we are shortly to get early airborne radar warning by Nimrods, which will mean that they won't be able to sneak in again† . . . .

Thatcher and Nott . . . have stepped up this war . . . . The principle is fine, but . . . world pressure and economic sanctions should have been enough [to induce Argentina to withdraw]. I cannot believe that Britain, after the experience of the First World War, can be starting another: but this is what Thatcher and Nott are doing. I just hope that the UN, USA and EEC have the humanity and wisdom to say: "Stop fighting, and let's sort this out peacefully". It is, after all, only a rock with a village population on it: more people live in Craven Arms!‡ Let us hope that by the time this letter gets to you they will have come to their senses and stopped the fighting.

Anyway, we are all fine here, and the paperwork has definitely subsided. I am now getting through all the books I

---

* Where did this bit of misinformation come from? David believed that Argentina had four Exocets: the press in Britain alleged five. In reality they had many more. Was this MOD trying to maintain morale?
† Dave soon discovered that the Nimrod story was yet another of MOD's fables: see his letter of 22 May.
‡ The nearest shopping centre to Clungunford in Shropshire.

brought out for the deployment to the Gulf but never got to read, and have plenty left as well. Sherlock Holmes is busy solving cases and Jeeves is proving almost as wise as Owl. I think that we should convert the hangar into a tennis court now that the season is coming on: more like a curling rink out here, but the weather at the moment is very calm and foggy, very much like November in England. A bit of a chill in the air, but no frost yet.

*To Christine*                    HMS GLAMORGAN, *13 May 1982*

Life must be very hard and worrying for you at present, but you need not worry over me. We have been securely in the main body of the Task Force all week, and it has been very quiet. Even the alarums and excursions are getting less. There was one yesterday when they came to about 100 miles away (the day *Brilliant* tested out Seawolf and shot down two planes). Otherwise, nothing at all has come anywhere near for the past week. We are still sitting at the edge of the [exclusion] zone. the more modern ships with their space-invader machines do all the zapping inshore.

All my love to you, Christine, at this difficult and sad time. I shall be back before too long to give you support.

*To H and E*    HMS GLAMORGAN, *14 May 1982 [received 28 May]*

Thank you for your nice long letter about events at home. You say that there isn't much news, but in fact it is very good to hear about events that are entirely peaceful and normal. You are quite right about people turning to Jane Austen in a war because nothing happened in her novels. I am reading a very long book where nothing happens at all, and very relaxing it is too.

The newspapers all seem to be screaming War, War and it must be the same on TV and radio. They give the impression that the whole of Britain is under attack . . . . It has been going on for two weeks now, but it seems ages. What did six years of World War II seem like? We are still eating well, etc., but everything is rationed and we tuck in heartily to cabbage and swedes as the only fresh veg that will keep on board.

I had a dream last night that I was back in the barracks in Portsmouth, that there was bread and spreads for tea, and the newsagents round the corner had unlimited supplies of sweets and today's newspapers. When I woke up, I thought "What a silly dream: that's not true any more . . . is it?" It will seem amazing when we get home that there isn't any war around. From the way that Maggie Thatcher has reacted one would imagine that the Russians were already in Bonn: not that we were fighting for a rocky island which Mr Nott had planned to leave completely undefended by mid-April! Maybe if Mark Thatcher were to drive his racing car in South America Mrs Thatcher would direct the whole navy to look for him (or consider the whole business much too dangerous and call it off).

The sad thing about all this is that everyone knows the complete hypocrisy of the government: which will never garrison the island sufficiently to defend it after this is all over, and is only fighting the war for its own political survival . . . .

[Then, family problems are mentioned.]

Not very cheering news to end the letter I'm afraid. Down here, we are now taking more precautions to safeguard our ship, keeping out of the way during daylight and good weather when the Argentinians can fly and only operating at night or bad weather when they can't. At least, with all these ships coming out we should be returning before too long. *They* can do the cleaning up afterwards.

Hope you are both keeping well and that Mrs Brush is enjoying her chicken (lucky cat).


*To Christine*                    HMS GLAMORGAN, *20 May 1982*


This letter should come to you by the next ship sailing home after *British Esk*. This is *HMS Leeds Castle*, a fishery protection vessel which is doing a postman's job for the Fleet between us and Ascension Island . . . . We have now been joined by some more ships and are even further away from the Falklands:

about eighty miles outside the exclusion zone. It is nice to know that the day will not be interrupted by alarms. My time at the moment is really rather gentlemanly. I get up about 8 a.m., have a leisurely breakfast, then come back [to the cabin], have a good wash, and wash my clothes, clean shoes, etc. It's rather good sleeping in your clothes. All the hassle about facing getting up is done away with! Anyway, about 10 I go down to the office, do all my paperwork in about half an hour, come back and have elevenses, and then read *Punch* until lunch. After lunch, some zedds maybe or perhaps on watch on the Flight Deck where I sit and read my Thomas Mann book, which I started in 1975, which is jolly intellectual. But more often I look out over the sea at all the ships around, and the birds, and the seaweed drifting by. The other day we saw some seals. They looked quite like dolphins, the way they arched through the water; but they were only half the size and all furry. I thought they just basked in the sun on some rocks. Still, I suppose they have to go fishing sometime . . . .

It has mostly been quite calm and often foggy, but I am still looking forward to seeing an iceberg appear. It is much better than off the Shetlands, where we usually are! There have been days when it's been very bright and brisk, and very colourful with the bright sun, green sea, and lovely white horses blown up into crests in the breeze. We look forward to the rough weather anyway, because it stops anyone from doing anything. And after eight weeks at sea it's a very soothing, rocking motion. I snuggle into a corner of my bed and wedge myself in, while the ship rocks me to sleep. You'll be glad to know that all this good living is making me nice and tubby (yuck). In the first week when it was all a bit hairy we all lost weight, and I became a very slim 28 inch waist. But it's all coming back on again now. In addition, now that they are rationing chocolate bars it make it absolutely imperative to have one, when I normally never bother!

I bet you have lost a lot of weight over the last few weeks. Poor Christine: it's worse for you because you don't know what the plans are, whereas at least we are in the know. And there is no point in my telling you, here, because it will be two-weeks-old news by the time this letter reaches you.

I suppose that by the time I get back you will have finished running in your new car . . . . I think it was very clever of you to get an extra £200 for DOF. Doubtless we shall see her chugging around the Shropshire lanes from time to time . . . . Thinking of the days when you used to go hurtling down hill sides on your bicycle (happy days) I've read in the papers that they are producing an electric bicycle . . . . This could be the way to get you out cycling again. Shropshire hills, here we come!

I gather that Sue Morgan phoned you up the other day to make contact. Owen and I, as you probably know, are on the Flight Deck together. They are both very nice people. Owen is very unassuming in what he's done: he's a Fellow of the Royal Society . . . . I went round to dinner with them on the night before we sailed. They had only moved into the quarter two days previously, which shows how very nice they both are . . . .

Well, this is the end of my writing pad. It will be scruffy letters from now on: maybe home-made envelopes!

*To H*          HMS GLAMORGAN, *22 May 1982 [received, 10 June]*

Your long marvellous letter of 6 May arrived today via *HMS Leeds Castle* (a most inappropriate name for a ship!) which is acting as postman between us and Ascension Island. It was like a breath of sanity coming into this totally mad world here. I am glad that you think that way about Mrs Thatcher and the war – as I have come to think since this business started. I sometimes wonder if I am totally odd in that I utterly oppose all this killing that is going on over a flag. Wilfred Owen wrote that "There'll come a day when men make war on death for lives, not men for flags",* but it has been the reverse here – "nations trek from progress" still.

It is quite easy to see how the war has come about; Mrs Thatcher imagined she was Churchill defying Hitler, and the Navy advised a quick war before the winter set in; the Navy chiefs also wanted maximum use made of the Navy for maximum publicity to reverse the Navy cuts: which has happened. For [utmost] worth, victory or defeat would have the same result; publicity and popular support, either con-

* From "The Next War".

gratulations or sympathy. The Navy thus overlooked the fact that we were fighting without all the necessary air cover which is provided by the USA in the Atlantic and by the RAF in the North Sea and Icelandic Sea. Although the Harrier is a marvellous little aircraft it is not a proper strike aircraft, and the best the Navy could get when carriers were "abolished". Consequently, we have no proper carriers which can launch early-warning aircraft fitted with radar as strike aircraft. From the Fifties onwards these two were absolute essentials.

However, the Navy felt that we were British and they [the Argentinians] were wogs, and that would make all the difference. The Admiral said as much to us on [the task force] TV. Consequently, we have no way of spotting low level attacks beyond 20 miles, which is how *Sheffield* was sunk. In a grandiose statement after the *Sheffield* loss, Nott stated that the Nimrod aircraft (early warning) and more Seawolf Type 22 frigates (which can shoot down Exocet) would be sent to the Falklands to counter this situation. Total lies! There is only one more Type 22 frigate and Nimrods have not appeared – even if fitted with in-flight refuelling gear it would be a difficult job for them. The only way we can counter these missiles is to keep out of range, which is what we have had to do.

Apart from the military fiasco the political side is even more disgraceful. Even if Britain does reconquer the Falklands we still have to talk to the Argentinians and come to some arrangement, so why not settle before a war has devastated the Falklanders' island? However, if Britain is going to turn the Falklands into a garrison island (in direct contravention of the Antarctic treaty?) it will show the complete hypocrisy of the British government which was going to leave the islands totally undefended and take away the islanders' British citizenship!* I suppose Mrs Thatcher will have to let them become British again – if so, will we provide them with a proper British health service, money for development, etc.? The garrison alone, with married quarters, NAAFI, hospital, barracks, air base, naval base, repair facilities, etc., bringing in, say, 3,000 people at the minimum (including dependants) will have to be taken out of NATO – so more defence spending

---

* After the 1981 Nationality Act the Falklanders were barred from settlement in the United Kingdom.

when the RN is to be cut by a third! Or, maybe, not cut the RN after all this publicity, and increase defence spending by, say, a third. The forces will have an immense mill stone around their necks; people will not want to go there (going to Scotland is hated enough) and the NCOs and Senior Ratings will simply leave the forces. The whole business is absolute nonsense.

I read that Argentina was prepared to accept a deal which involved Argentinian sovereignty and British administration and way of life. Those, to me, sound fair terms to avoid bloodshed. Now that war has started, neither side can give way until the other is exhausted. This is not a war between civilised countries. It is not fought for any good reason (trade, survival, top-nation status etc.) but is fought on a "principle" by two dictatorships. It is a dangerous state of affairs in Britain when the Prime Minister can tell the forces to go to war without consulting even Parliament. If that is the case, it is time the forces were cut so that it is impossible to use them for anything but the defence of Britain, and [that] they were placed under NATO control. Thinking of wars fought on "principle" alone I can only think of religious wars of bigotry, and the Thirty Years War which destroyed Germany. Thinking of enormous expenditure, I can only think of the Spanish Armada, the Dutch Wars of Independence – and Suez! A classicist on board also quoted an example of another dying power having a last fling. I only hope that the Falklands do not become our Vietnam, but so long as this government is in power they will be . . . . Mrs Thatcher, and our Admiral (he, more understandably) seem to have no compunction about casualties at all – the initial shock of *Sheffield* has worn off, and now they are accepted willingly – 20 yesterday in a helicopter, and 20 in *Ardent*. And they will not end until one side surrenders.

I haven't mentioned much about the war and our part in it in my letters to Elisabeth and you, and to Christine, so as to try to avoid upsetting and worrying them in addition to the worry they must already feel, especially when the news is so regularly ghastly. However, I will to you, because you know what it's like; with six years' worth, it won't seem so unexpected. We still cannot believe we are at war, even while it's going on, and when I have had a good night's sleep I wake up without remembering the war for a while. Our surroundings, of course, are exactly as normal: and we are very used to doing perpetual exercises. We still have proper food, hot water to wash with, etc. There are a few differences; covers and fabrics have been thrown away, the scuttles (windows) permanently blacked out, the chests tied down, no loose papers about – but life has its flashes of normality. I sometimes have some typing to do, we have "Requestmen" and "Defaulters", the NAAFI sells chocolate, and we still have "Elevenses" (at Stand Easy). As we don't have personal weapons there's no particular feeling that we are fighting. We are mostly a peaceful bunch who would not want to shoot anyone. The war just happens; we do shelling of shore positions and we get attacked by aircraft. We dislike both, and the time when everyone is relaxed and happy is when we are "legging it" away from the action at 29 knots. On one such dash, 120 miles after the raid on Pebble Island, where the SAS and our guns destroyed aircraft on the ground (14 May) we used 33,000 gallons of fuel – 6 yards per gallon! We can always rely on the engineers to get us out as fast as possible. Blow the expense on fuel!

The actual war part of it is not so much frightening but tense. In the first week when the fleet was closer inshore (70 miles) and continually under air threat some people were getting to their "nerves' ends", especially those in the Operations Room where the war is fought from (all the radar screens, communications, and missile buttons are there, and they have to react quickly to air attack). However, after the *Sheffield* incident the Fleet moved further away out of range, and the alarms grew less. For three days we didn't go to action stations once (during the early stages of the UN peace moves) and people relaxed and came to terms with the situation. Yesterday [was] the landings-day, when five ships were badly damaged because they were positioned by the Admiral in the middle of the islands and could only pick up the attacking aircraft at about one or two miles (about 10-15 seconds reaction time). They were just sitting targets to the wave of four aircraft at a time coming over. They would have enough time to shoot maybe four shells out of a Seacat close-range missile, and would take out one or two of the four aircraft. Anyway, all the ships were damaged (we were out with the carriers, 100 miles away at the time) and we were ordered in to replace the other

County Class destroyer [*Antrim*] which had been written off: to sit in the middle of the channel and be attacked. It would have been certain damage for the ship, and it did feel like being sent over the top at the Somme. Fortunately, an hour later, the Admiral changed his plan and we didn't go in and it was decided to move the ships out.

We are all prepared for fighting at sea when we can at least engage the aircraft with Seaslug, our main system, with a range of 20 miles; but going inshore when you can only see the aircraft at a mile is just suicide.

We had in fact done this on the first day, 1 May, when we had the dubious privilege of being first into the Falklands with *Arrow* and *Alacrity*. We shelled Stanley airport while we were inside the minefield (!) about two miles off shore. Sure enough, we were attacked by two waves of four Mirages and it was too close before we had seen them to engage with Seaslug and they were flying too low, right behind us, [for us] to bring the Seacat or guns to bear (we saw them at one mile). Fortunately, they had a lot to do in that seven seconds and were probably a bit jumpy, so didn't hit us. They first strafed with cannon, dropped a bomb, and fired a rocket, one aircraft up each side of the ship, and one aircraft each for the two frigates. It wasn't particularly noisy – a lot of wooshes and some dacca-dacca. We had all [on the Flight Deck] legged it into the hangar and lay flat on the deck, tin helmets on and fingers in ears: so we didn't see anything – but heard it all. First, the screams of "Aircraft, Aircraft" over the armament broadcast; bangs as we fired chaff (plastic dog-hairs in clouds to produce false radar echoes), wooshes as all sixteen chaff-rockets were fired, then dacca-dacca from the aircraft, bang-bang as the bombs went off by the stern, lifting the screws right out of the water (we thought we'd been hit), then woosh-woosh as the rockets went past us. It was close, as we thought it was our own Seacat firing, about 20 feet away. Some more dacca-dacca (us and them) and two bangs from our guns as they [the planes] flew off. We then legged it! Maybe the pilots were put off by the enormous battle Ensigns we were flying from each mast (we're such traditionalists in County Class destroyers), a good Nelsonian touch: I don't think ships do that any more – after all the efforts we took to camouflage ourselves by painting all our white parts and our chrome parts grey! In addition, that day we were also trying to operate two helicopters on our [Flight] deck which only just takes one, and we did the most amazing things with them: launching them sideways, backwards, etc. When launching sideways the wheels fit on the deck with 1½ feet to play with on either side. Anyway, an exhausting day.

After that they decided that going inshore by day wasn't quite such a good idea and so after that we only went in at night when their aircraft couldn't fly. However, our Admiral didn't seem to know any other ships' names apart from *Glamorgan*, *Arrow*, and *Alacrity*. If anything came up, we would do it: bombarding, being detached to fight off hostile approaching ships, etc.: we became known as the Three Musketeers. We bombarded Stanley again that night and were detached to fight the "Northern Decoy Group" (two tugs/corvettes) which we attacked with helicopters. After *Sheffield's* loss, *Glamorgan* became the "Duty Exocet Target Ship": fifteen miles ahead of the force in the direction of the enemy. Things quietened down in the second week when the Admiral learnt some other names and hit on the idea of sending in a Type 22 Seawolf ship (4 miles range) and a Type 42 Seadart ship (40 miles range) inshore during daylight to go duck-shooting: a good idea as Seawolf will shoot down anything. However, this was given up when *Glasgow* was bombed. Although the bomb did not go off it severed the electricity, fuel, and air pipes, which put her out of action for a while, and the force was down to one Type 42 and us, as air defence. Therefore, for the third week, it was us again, and we went in to do raids and bombardment at night, [plus] Pebble Island on 14th May when the BBC were on board and grandiosed everything out of all proportion (Antarctic wind, Force 9 gales, terrific disruption done, disrupted entire Argentinian war effort, etc.). Mostly, they sat drinking the Wardroom beer and were sick in the Heads: the weather was in fact quite good.

After that it was bombarding Stanley, same place, same time, on the 16th, 18th, 19th and 20th May – *Glamorgan* only – we were a bit jumpy about going back there three nights in a row: surely they would get wise? But fortunately they did not react very much. On the BBC this was classed as a "dangerous mission . . . in a possible minefield". The Admiral said it would be a piece of cake. And no-one told us about the minefield. We did see the Argentinians firing at each other.

They were obviously jumpy. On the last night we lit ourselves up with flares: we all jumped for cover on the Flight Deck. Nobody had warned us this would happen as we were only a mile off the coast at the time, and similarly nobody told the engineers we were going to drop scare charges and they thought we were being torpedoed. The Chinese tailor leaped out of bed about three feet and had his clothes on in five seconds.

Anyway, we did a good job of scaring ourselves, if not the Argentinians, and the Admiral was pleased (and amazed?) that it had gone off safely. We had commenced these raids at a regulation 8 knots with super-duper modern anti-submarine countermeasures but by the end we used good old-fashioned zigzagging madly and steaming at 24 knots. We were mightily relieved when we legged it from our first "0230 to Port Stanley, calling at Stork Bay, Beacon Point and Beauchamp Channel".

That night the landings went in and it is now the second day that they have been ashore. Fortunately, the poor ships still in there have not been attacked today and should come out tomorrow. It has been a dreadful price in ships to pay – one ship for every four aircraft. If we could fight them in the open sea our chances would be so much better. I would much prefer that their air force just did *not* fight but it looks like the only way to end this will be to break the back of their air force (we have destroyed about fifty out of two hundred). Despite what the press and public opinion say, they are brave men who have to do their duty as we do.

I suppose that this sort of naval war is quite different from your war when you had to put up with a lot more . . . lasting for six years.* These last three weeks have seemed long enough and we don't like to think any more into the future than the end of the day. We are lucky in that we can rescue our survivors and send them back to England, and our living conditions are fine; but air attack by these very fast jets coming in low is not very nice.

The pity for us is that there is no cause for this war; and, to be honest, the Argentinians are more patriotic about the Malvinas than we are about the Falklands. And the iniquitous

* David is generous, but the war his father knew, 1939-45, was much less demanding.

thing is that we trained and equipped them! Their carrier, Type 42 destroyers, submarines and aircraft are all European. Britain even sold Argentina the maps of the Falklands a month before the invasion so that there were no maps for our own troops when we needed them. We were about to train their Lynx helicopter crews to use the Sea Skua missile (in May). That's the only advantage we have over their ships at present. And we even gave them an official cocktail party when one of their Type 42 destroyers was training in Portsmouth last year! I suppose we didn't think that we'd have a warmonger in charge. The first of Commander-in-Chief Fleet's *Classified Memoranda* (which all officers have to read) says: "As Britain will have no strike carrier from 1979 it is inherent that Britain should not go it alone in a future war but should fight under the NATO umbrella".

Still, I suppose this is all an experience one should go through if only to drive home for each generation how stupid war is. As Housman wrote:

> Ay, yonder lads are yet
>   The fools that we were then;
> For oh, the sons we get
>   Are still the sons of men.
> The sumless tale of sorrow
>   Is all unrolled in vain:
> May comes tomorrow
>   And Ludlow fair again.*

I suppose he would have approved of the irony of a war starting on May 1st: also the anniversary of Gallipoli!

Certainly the trivia of life and the important things are all brought to mind by this. And how much the trivia are at the forefront of normal life and the important things put away, or not done, or left to do later and then forgotten. Here, certainly, the material things are unimportant and human "things", values, and ways of life are thought about by everybody.

* From "The First of May" (*Last Poems*).


*To Christine*                          HMS GLAMORGAN, *23 May 1982*

How I love you: so very much. You are absolutely wonderful. You have been very brave indeed over the past weeks, and I am very proud of you. You seem to be standing up to it so very well: much better than the other wives and it really heartens me to know that you are not letting it get you down too much. Although I know and feel for you, that you have been going through agonies over the casualty and damage reports from the landings. It has been about three days since they first gave details of casualties, and even now they haven't said who, and which ships (I hope that's because they informed next of kin *first* this time and didn't just bleat it out over the news). It has been a horrible time for you, and I have been feeling for you all through it. We were 100 miles away from the landings with the carriers, and nothing came out to us. I am glad that Captain Barrow sent a signal . . . to say what was going on, but I was saddened to see that he opened with news of "blasting the Argies" and I had to read it twice to spot that he said we weren't in the area and were OK . . . .

We are acting as carrier guardship with the main force, 100 miles from the Falklands and out of range of Argentine aircraft so that the carriers are secure. Now that the Rapier missile systems are established there is no need for the ships to remain close in, apart from the landing ships which come out once they have off-loaded their gear. I think that the troops will appreciate being able to fight a proper battle, particularly the Paras, Marines, and Gurkhas. They can now work out the aggression they have had to bottle up in Ireland; and for the Gurkhas, of course, it is the highest point of honour to be in battle, and they will go back to their villages as proud men. I think the Guards are there for the peace celebrations and the QE2 was the only possible ship . . . . I am convinced they have their scarlet tunics with them! Seriously, the Guards have always been very solid in battle. I do hope that the Argentinian soldiers surrender before too long. They have already proved their bravery honourably, and there is no need to prolong it.

I had your lovely letters today from 3-5 May . . . . I really liked hearing about the happenings at Clungunford. Isn't it lovely that the geese have a little yellow chick and Mrs has two little lambs – she is clever. Little animals are so sweet – why is it that human babies are so repulsive? . . . .

I don't blame you for not wanting to leave home after the bank holiday. It is a cold and difficult time for you at the moment with your mother ill and your family worried, and me away . . . . Just keep going from day to day as we all do, and eventually it will be over. I am very proud of you, Christine. You are a girl in a million, and you're mine and I love you. Nothing is more important than our love which can't be hurt by anything. It has grown stronger and stronger over the past five years we've been together, and it will stand the test of anything. It is unassailable. It gives me total fulfilment and happiness in life which I never had before I met you, and I know it is the same for you. When we are together again I will be able to comfort you, console you, and love you. But even now that we are apart it's still there, with a confidence and a warm glow. It is complete, ultimate, and assured. It is a perfect and pure love that lasts for ever.

*To Gordon and Marion Hayes*    HMS GLAMORGAN, *25 May 1982*

Thank you for your letter from the beginning of the month . . . . In contrast to your frantic schedule my routine has now become very leisurely, as no-one is interested in paperwork any more. My action station is on the Flight Deck where it is most refreshing to see the world and the wildlife: of which there is plenty, including beautiful albatrosses following in the wake so effortlessly . . . . Out here it is just like November: some lovely crisp clear days with a shining sun and people's breath steaming. Other times there is a silent, close fog with the sea very still. The sea is much calmer here than round UK and the myth of terrific storms battering the Fleet has been created by the press who, when they came to stay with us, spent most of the time feeling seasick, poor people. However, I suppose in July the weather will be much worse.

*Glamorgan* has had quite an active time during May. We had the dubious privilege of being the first ship into the Falklands . . . . We had all thought that war was only a question of pressing buttons but it is still very much a hit and miss affair. The number of unexploded bombs that have landed in ships over the last few days has been incredible (and fortunate). The Royal Marines, strapped to the exposed small 20 mm guns on the Signal Deck, enjoyed it terrifically. One shouted "Come here and let me get you, you so and so". I can't say that we were so brave. We legged it into the hangar . . . .

Our other main task was to go in nightly . . . on our own, to shell Stanley and the coast south of there to make it look as if we were preparing to invade there. We did this on May 16th, 18th, 19th and 20th . . . . Now is a good time to buy BP shares as we used to run in and out, 150 miles each way per day. On our return from the Pebble Island raid . . . we had to return 120 miles with only three hours of darkness left. The engineers gave it all they had and we used 33,000 gallons of fuel: six yards per gallon!

It is a very odd feeling being at war out here. We are so used to exercises that it is not particularly different, only much more tense. In our nightly raids, the tension would slowly build up, and when we came away at high speed the relief would be enormous, almost euphoric. People would be smiling and making jokes and relaxing. Certainly, for me, seeing the Falklands disappearing over the horizon behind an enormous wake is very satisfying! We have no feeling of "fighting". The war just happens. We fire our guns and we get attacked and in between we try to carry on our lives at sea as if nothing had happened . . . .

Of course, what is happening here must feel familiar to you from the Second World War:* the bravery and courage of our own pilots, flying an aircraft which was designed simply to intercept Soviet reconnaissance aircraft and which is now being pitted against supersonic fighters and used for bombing with gear little more advanced than the Lancaster. And the bravery and tragic waste of life of the Argentinian pilots, sent against overwhelming anti-aircraft missiles by heartless superiors. The devotion to duty of our frigates in the Falklands Sound, who were sitting ducks for the Argentinian aircraft and which were all hit by bombs. And above all, the tragedy, anguish, and horror of the British lives that have been lost: which have been spent quite willingly by Mrs Thatcher and Mr Nott to make up for the political ineptitude and pigheadedness of the Government. When one considers the total of sorrow, financial loss, loss of ships for Britain (which I doubt will ever be replaced) and destruction to the Falklands

* When Gordon was in the Royal Navy.

– now dotted with war graves – all balanced against a "principle", a flag, and the ousting of two dozen islanders [those expelled] it does seem to me personally the most pointless of wars ever fought by Britain.

I had hoped that our Government would compromise, to bring a peaceful settlement: but now the only way to end this, for the time being, will be to defeat the Argentinians, and I hope that they surrender soon. They have proved their bravery, honourably, already. Of course once we regain the islands we will still have to talk to the Argentinians, unless we want to provide a garrison of three soldiers for every inhabitant. The Falklands will end up much better defended than the UK!

Anyway, I will look forward to seeing you again before too long and my very best wishes until then.*

* Gordon and Marion are Clungunford friends. David's letter to them is actually much longer, but some of the things he wrote are also included in the other letters he wrote just before and after this one.

*To Jonathan and Helena*          HMS GLAMORGAN, *28 May 1982*
                                 *[received, 21 June]*

Thank you very much for writing. I received your letter via the "reinforcements" which arrived a couple of days ago. It is very nice to know that you are thinking of us and I appreciate your thoughts.

Although you say it seems very unreal in England it's also very unreal here. Even when, on the first day, we had just been attacked by their Mirages we were saying to each other that it couldn't be real. Why were we fighting *Argentina*? And who wanted to live here [in the Falklands] anyway?

I cannot think of a single war in Britain's history which has been so pointless. They have always been either for trade, survival, maintaining the balance of power, world [economic?] growth, etc. This one is to recapture a place which we were going to leave undefended from April, and to deprive its residents of British citizenship in October. And to recapture it, having built up *their* forces with the most modern Western arms (not even *we* have the air-launched Exocet which is so deadly). And fighting ourselves without the two pre-requisites of naval warfare: air cover, and airborne early warning, which have been essential since World War II . . . .

Not only has Mrs Thatcher survived a political fiasco; she has covered up the military cost to Britain (ten times what it will cost the Argentinians) and sent a fleet to do a job it should never have been sent to do: because of no air cover resulting in four ships sunk, four written off, and more damaged. She has become a complete dictator, ordering war without consulting Parliament, and she is dragging the masses, shouting and cheering, behind her. The newspapers just see it as a real-life "War Mag", and even have drawings of battles, and made-up descriptions, entirely from their own imagination! If some of the horrible ways that people have died occurred in *their* offices maybe they would change their tone. Let us just hope it ends quickly.

If we do recapture the islands we will still have to talk to the Argentinians, and I doubt if Mrs Thatcher will compromise at all: in which case we will have to provide a garrison of about three Servicemen to every one inhabitant and spend millions of pounds on all the military installations that will be necessary and keep at least a submarine, two ships, a squadron of aircraft, AA missiles, a radar early warning system, anti-ship land-based missiles, and a garrison of soldiers there. They will need married quarters, sickbay, school, NAAFI, etc. The whole thing is totally ludicrous.

What Mrs Thatcher does not realise is that the Argentinians *believe* that the Malvinas are theirs. They have sent pilots on suicide missions against us, on a one-way journey, because we are out of their range: so they effectively double the range of their aircraft by not going back. And they don't have any sea-rescue helicopters to pick up the pilots afterwards. In fact, the bravery of all their pilots shows that they are more than "mildly" interested in the Falklands.

The sad thing about all this, of course, is that the professional forces of both sides (not the conscripts) do what they are told. So if two megalomaniac idiots tell them to beat each other's brains out, they do; and there is no stopping them. Our own frigates were ordered into a similar suicidal position in Falkland Sound and stayed there until ordered out again, after 80 per cent were sunk or badly damaged. I am sure the troops of both sides are a peaceloving lot (although I do wonder about the Paras and the Marines) and the news we listen for is that of peace moves, not damage inflicted on the enemy. That, we regard as unfortunately necessary because it is the only way to end this business, which our political masters have sent us into with such glee.

I must admit that I am disappointed in the actions of Dr Runcie [the Archbishop of Canterbury], both in stopping the Bishop of Argentina from coming to the Falklands to tell them that the Argentinians didn't actually have horns on their heads and in approving of this war in a "St George and the Dragon" way. But I suppose as he won an MC he thinks fighting for a just cause is OK. However, I am pleased to see that both the Liberals and the Baptists oppose war and advocate peaceful means. There are "more ways to kill a cat than choking it with cream" and I believe that trade sanctions and world opinion should have been enough. It is not as if the Argentinians killed anyone, and now we have decided to go in heavy-handed about four hundred people are dead (including a hundred British) and it must have cost the UK about £1 billion so far (ships come out at about £150 million, planes, £10 million: people are cheaper). It will all end up with the equivalent of handing over a million pounds to each Falklander, and burning the money . . . .

But enough of my sarcasm. They really should not send people in the Services to study history at university. The Captain, who is a very peaceloving and Christian man, and who has been in the Navy since the age of thirteen, just says things about democracy, and duty, and resisting invasion . . . .

We seem to have settled into our way of life out here now, which isn't too different from normal. We still have hot water to wash in, copies of *Punch* to read, films, ample food, and a bed to sleep in at night. Much more comfortable than the poor old soldiers! One nice thing is that we sleep in our clothes so getting up in the morning is really easy! Paperwork has also subsided which is good. I spend quite a lot of time on watch on the Flight Deck which is very pleasant as I usually read a book, and look out over the sea at all the ships and the wildlife and enjoy the fresh air. The weather is just like the UK around here, and it is only just now starting to turn wintry. *Not* the huge gales that the press say there are.

We tend to live from day to day here and don't look too far

ahead. In the first week of it all, when things were quite hot, people were very tense, and everyone lost a lot of weight. However, the UN peace negotiations brought a lull, when everybody adjusted to the situation. After that, most of the action was around the bridgehead, while we were out with the carriers. We have done quite a number of night raids and bombardments, but their aircraft haven't been flying at night, so that eases the adrenilin a bit. We don't like aircraft: especially the ones with the horrid missiles! Every time a ship is sunk by Exocet, the Chinese in the laundry all get twitched and pack their bags and say they are leaving. We humour them by letting them put their bags in the hangar, and let them stand around on the Flight Deck for a bit, waiting for a helicopter to take them away. After a while, they calm down again and go back to work. Poor people.

Anyway, we are all looking forward to the Gurkhas doing their bit and clearing out the Argentinians from Stanley. Once the runway is in use again it will make life much easier. Stores can be flown in: air defence equipment and missiles, fighter planes, more troops, etc. Then it will just be a question of mopping up resistance from the army, and keeping the Argentinian planes at a distance. The naval and air war could go on forever though, to some degree; until either they lose all their ships, submarines and planes or Galtieri & Co get the boot. I'm sure someone will benefit from all this destruction, even though it is only Mrs Thatcher and the arms manufacturers!

Hope Stretford is going well. I'm glad to hear all about the news of your cottage and sailing: which reminds me, it's Summer, isn't it? See you when I get back, eventually.


*To Christine*                          HMS GLAMORGAN, *30 May 1982*


I received two lovely letters from you today dated 17 May – only 13 days, that's very quick . . . they came down with the QE2 . . . . Today we had a chance to send off a *Familygram*, so I have sent one off to you with the added cheek of asking for a "Red Cross Parcel". I hope you don't mind: and I hope it's a big one! It is a bit like boarding school here: people receive Red Cross Parcels here with great whoops of joy, proudly displaying the contents, while everyone else looks on with great admiration at the goodies brought out – they almost seem from another planet.

Also, for today and tomorrow, we have moved outside the [exclusion] zone to a holding area, where the tugs are also, incidentally. It is a very nice feeling to be out of it for a while – most relaxing – the only thing that has come over this way has been the odd Argentinian Hercules. We have, of course, got used to being in the zone, and life on board is really quite normal. The Captain even phones me up in the hangar to ask if I have anything for him to sign. Unfortunately, the NAAFI has sold just about everything – even tins of Spam to the sailors. The Canteen Manager has a very captive and willing market but unfortunately the poor man has only got the shelves left to sell: otherwise he would have become Salesman of the Year (anyone who can sell Spam to well-fed sailors is doing very well indeed!). However, we still have films on board which get changed round regularly, and because we are in the zone now we get the really modern ones which are currently showing in the cinemas (it makes the mass-produced Holly-wood stuff seem more palatable somehow) . . . .

It's now about midnight, and I have started to wake up. Because of our night-time usual activities we tend to be quite drowsy during the day and all awake at night! And if you go and have soup and bread at the watch change at 0200 hours you can stay awake quite happily until 0500 and not feel sleepy at all. Often when you are sleeping in short phases you can't remember whether it's day or night when you wake up. If the clock says 6 o'clock, for example, you have to think back to what the time was when you went to sleep, and then count forward. It's quite nice with three of us in the Flight Deck roster because it demands enough of your time to prevent you working set hours in the office. I usually turn up at 10 a.m. and work half an hour – even an hour some days! This gives you enough time off to spend as much time asleep as you like. Even when we are "On Watch" we don't have to be on deck if nothing at all is happening. The sun rises here about 11 o'clock and sets about 8 p.m. (We are still on Greenwich Mean Time: much simpler all round). So if I have the afternoon watch I often go out on deck to see the world, read a book, and take the air. It has started to get wintry now, and the wind is definitely cold . . . just like early December in Britain. The latitude here is about the same as London. It will be very odd having three Christmasses in the space of thirteen months.

We have some pet seagulls on the Flight Deck now. They are all white and look a bit like doves when flying . . . . They have been following us around for about five days now. One is very friendly and eats bread out of the PO Aircrewman's hand and is quite jealous of his favoured position and sometimes chases the others away . . . . The other seagull is a very pure white, but he hasn't quite mastered deck landings yet in a cross-wind. When he lands, he almost takes off again, and bounces around from leg to leg, stretching out very long toes to keep his balance: rather an inexperienced pilot, though. I often feel he needs tying down with the nylon lashings, like the helicopter, to keep him on deck. He is a bit more timid than the other, but quite happily eats the bread we leave out for him. They are usually both to be seen strutting round the Flight Deck, pecking at this and that, and investigating all the corners and cosy holes. They haven't yet started nesting in the hangar!

We have been hearing recently on the News of 2 Battalion Parachute Regiment's brilliant attack on Darwin and Goose Green. This must rate as one of the most outstanding infantry actions in history – on a par with Clive at Plassey. Attacking at odds of one to three, when it should have been three to one . . . is utterly incredible. It must have been a dreadfully fierce battle with 250 Argentine dead. I hope the Argentinians' willingness to fight and accept such losses makes the press at home treat them with more respect. As ever, those furthest from the front jeer and jibe the loudest, have the most bravado, and urge war the most. I'm sure C-in-C Fleet in his concrete bunker 8,000 miles away is loving every minute of it . . . . I know our Admiral isn't enjoying it particularly.

Also emerging is that the poor islanders have had their homes looted: but I think we knew that would be inevitable. With ten soldiers for every inhabitant on the island, what can one expect? I am sure they will be jolly glad to have the Union Jack back and drive on the left-hand side of the road (especially round Stanley where they have actually got roads).* Anyway,

* After 150 years of British colonial rule there were eight miles of motorable road outside Stanley.

I must stop being cynical or else they will court-martial me for spreading Argentine propaganda or discouraging people from fighting each other or something wicked like that.

Must stop now. My knees are getting sore. Since my chair is tied to the towel rail [all moveable objects were lashed down] I have to write letters by kneeling at my desk. Now I know how Jonathan feels!


*To Christine*                          HMS GLAMORGAN, *5 June 1982*

Last time I wrote we had just moved to the maintenance area for 48 hours: and we are still here a week later! All our maintenance has been done but we have organised a nice little niche for ourselves here, in managing all the supply ships, getting them in the right station, organising whom and from whom they should fuel, delivering their mail and stores to them with helicopters, etc. We've even conned the Admiral so well that although our helicopter isn't working we have borrowed another ship's; and do their stores transfers with it. We are now known as *RFA Glamorgan.**

The area out here, well to the east of the carrier group, is known as the TRALA (something like "Tug [or Transit?], Repair, and Logistics Area") and very tra-la-la it is too. We haven't been to action stations all week and at night don't even bother with defence watches. It has been a great tonic for everyone, especially for those who had been working straight one-in-two watches (i.e. on-off, on-off) for the whole of [this] last month and the last part of April. Life has returned to the Wardroom, people are smiling and making jokes, reading the papers and watching the film in the evening. Usually, the Wardroom is deserted except for meal times, when everyone is changing watches, and the only people you'll find there are layabout Flight Deck Officers. However, I'm disturbed that some of the junior ratings and single officers actually want to go back into the [operational] area (I shall have to suppress these mutinous tendencies).

Actually, the Fleet down here has changed quite a lot and there are only a few of the old hands left: it gives us a sort of

* Royal Fleet Auxiliary (the merchant ships of the Royal Navy)

"Out since Mons" air and especially when the reinforcements come down and are always at action stations when we are steaming about normally! Just to give you an idea, this is what has happened to the original Fleet:

| | |
|---|---|
| *Hermes/Invincible:* | Both still in the [operational] area |
| *Glamorgan:* | TRALA area |
| *Antrim:* | South Georgia; undergoing repairs from D-day damage |
| *Glasgow:* | Returning to UK after unexploded bomb damage |
| *Sheffield:* | Sunk on 4 May |
| *Coventry:* | Sunk on 25 May |
| *Broadsword/Brilliant:* | Both still in area: both damaged and will need repairs in UK (in time) |
| *Arrow:* | In San Carlos Bay: will need to return to UK: split hull from *Sheffield* knocking [into her] |
| *Alacrity:* | Returning to UK: mechanical problems |
| *Plymouth/Yarmouth:* | Both in San Carlos Bay: will need to return for maintenance in UK |

And also the first wave of replacements:

| | |
|---|---|
| *Argonaut:* | Returning to UK: bomb damage |
| *Ardent:* | Sunk 21 May |
| *Antelope:* | Sunk 21 May |

– which is why we don't have first call on returning to UK.

There *is* a good train of thought, to which I subscribe, which says that we ought to return first because we have the least to fix (boiler clean, and various bits which need regular replacing, evaporators, etc). This is because the plan is for the first lot to return mid-June and leave UK again by the end of August: hopefully having relieved the Captain and his Secretary!

There was a report in the press on about 2 June saying that *Glamorgan* would be returning first because of bomb damage – total fabrication. *Antrim* is the one damaged by the bomb. They are dreadful, the press: they just make these things up when they haven't got solid facts to work on – like the *Sunday Times* account of the Pebble Island [raid] which said "This is what it was probably like" – and then gave graphic detail – all of which was wrong. Anyway I know these press reports must be horribly alarming but they are just not true. The most blatant one is the weather, which they say is foul, but which is much better than UK.

I don't like writing about the war to you but just for the record I suppose I should let you know what we did so you aren't fed untrue tit-bits.

| | |
|---|---|
| 1 May: | Shelled Stanley airport with *Arrow* and *Alacrity*, close inshore, inside the minefield – during daylight. Attacked by eight Mirages – low, and only seen at a mile; bombs dropped near the stern lifting the ship out of the water; rockets fired down the side of the ship; cannon fire. No damage done .... Returned at night to shell the airport again (aircraft could not fly at night). |
| 2 May: | Argentine pincer naval attack: northern group of two corvettes to decoy British ships from main group and attack them during day. We were surface group commander, but were [sent] south to shell Stanley again and helicopters sank the corvettes with Sea Skua during the night (and *Belgrano* sank to the south). Consequently, we were not required. |
| 4 May: | *Sheffield* sunk in main group: nobody else knew she had been hit until an hour later (she lost all communications). A worrying time. |
| 6 and 8 May: | Bombarding Stanley again at night (1-12 May, action stations frequently, about three times per day). |
| 6 to 21 May: | UN talks, and lessening of activity in the area. |
| 14 May: | Pebble Island raid with *Hermes*. We destroyed eight aircraft by gunfire. The SAS took out an ammunition dump (huge orange glow in the night) and three aircraft with plastic explosives. A very moonlit night – jumpy. High-speed escape from 0830: all engines flat out. The ship's wake was as broad as a motorway! |
| 16, 18, 19, 20 May: | Bombarding Stanley again at night: *their* shells landed 200 yards away. Final night, we dropped scare charges and illuminated ourselves with flares – we scared ourselves more than the Argentinians. |

| 21 May: | D-Day. Because of the daily bombardment we were not put into the area. All the ships were hit: two sunk and two written off, a dreadful day, as we heard the news coming in. We would have been in *Antrim's* place had not the Admiral transferred to us before Ascension, and *Antrim* had gone to South Georgia. *Antrim* was bombed and strafed. Evening of 21 May: we were ordered into the area to replace *Antrim*: an awful couple of hours before the Admiral changed his mind and decided that he couldn't afford to lose any more ships. *Coventry* was ordered in instead, to a different, more open sea area, to act as a "Missile Trap" and was of course sunk four days later. |
|---|---|
| 25 May: | (*Coventry* sunk inshore) An Exocet attack with about five seconds warning. *Atlantic Conveyer*, the biggest ship in the force sunk. We bombarded Stanley again that night in retaliation, and launched our Seaslug at the runway (they don't go off on the surface: it is just a gesture). |
| 26, 28 May: | Night bombardment again with *Ambuscade* and *Avenger*. Shells fell to fifty yards of us. We launched two more Seaslugs. Frightened us more than them. We have now fired 1000 4·5″ shells. |
| 30 May: | Exocet attack again. Forty-five seconds warning this time, and we got into position (bows towards missile) and fired chaff . . . . However, missile came towards us and we braced for impact. Missile either went into a wave, or into some chaff, or ran out of gas, quarter of a mile from us. Phew! ! |
| 30 May: | Full speed ahead for the TRALA: and here we are. |

Over this period, the mood and feeling on board have changed from being very tense to becoming used to the situation. The attacks are not particularly frightening, they are over so quickly. However, one always has to be prepared to go to Action Stations and to expect this and that: and that is the main difference to life. It is an odd feeling being attacked: a mixture of "Goodbye, cruel world", as you lie there with tin helmet on, braced for it: and a feeling that "They must be mad. Don't they know it's very unsafe shooting things at other people?" One is always so conscious of safety, normally, you just cannot imagine somebody doing something as deliberately unsafe as pointing it at anyone – and pressing the button. The best thing to do is to have a few wets before an attack. I'd had a drink before the Exocet attack and the pulse rate stayed very normal, although when "Brace, Brace, Brace" came over the broadcast* I did think to myself "Expletive deleted". They had it worst in the Ops Room where they could see it coming towards us – the Ops Officer said his heart almost pounded itself out of its rib cage. Poor man: ignorance is bliss on these occasions.

Now, of course, the mood on board is very relaxed, and very nice it is too. We have just gone back to "1 in 4", cruising watches. Living day to day, one tries to make times when everything is going very well indeed – like when coming off watch in the evening, when nothing is planned for the night, or when some mail has come and there's a Mars Bar saved up to eat, or just when there's no work looming and some time to read a book; when the Falklands are disappearing behind us at a great rate of knots after a raid, or when we are out of the way in the TRALA. In such times I feel a sense of "well being", as now when I've just had a Mars Bar and am writing to you.

These times are getting more frequent now that we're out here with the supply ships, and it is nice to have them; easier to do living on a day to day basis, when it's just the present that is important – and the present's OK. In the same way one looks forward to meal times, and having a beer, and that sort of thing: the sort of thing one just accepts, normally, and concentrates on the horrid part of life, i.e. work!

One of our jobs out here is to transfer stores around between ships and yesterday I walked into the hangar and found a nuclear bomb there. I suppose if the USA and USSR have got 7,000 each, the chance of walking into one must be increased, but nevertheless I was rather surprised, and wondered if it was worth sheltering in the hangar any more. Of course, it turned out to be a drill round, full of concrete, that *Fort Austin*, now eventually going home was taking back to England. I don't really know why we brought any down here. Loosing one off really would evaporate support for us by the EEC and

* Brace against the missile's impact.

Third World. Anyway, at least this lump of concrete is going back.

[Then small personal details follow.]

My dear Christine, how I love you, so very much: and think of you much of the time. Thinking of you makes me feel happy, and I often have dreams where we are off in your new car, doing lots of fun things, and having great adventures. It doesn't feel that you are very far away; for all I know, Portsmouth is just over the horizon. It's not very different down here, as it is at home, although I can't imagine it is summer somehow, and seeing cricket in the papers is very odd. I'm looking forward to when I can put my dreams into practice . . . .

*To H and E*                          HMS GLAMORGAN, *8 June 1982*
                                       *[received 30 June]*

It seems quite some time since I wrote to you last; I have now received your letters up to 17 May. Thank you very much for them. It is very nice indeed to hear news of the normal world as one has to look very hard in the papers to find anything that is not about war.

On 30 May we moved eighty miles to the east away from the carrier group to the TRALA area . . . . We are now, would you believe, in cruising watches – I think there's someone somewhere looking out for the Argentinians. This break from defence watches . . . has been a great relief for the Operations Room people, as we had been in defence watches continuously since April 21st: when we were still 2,000 miles away from the Falklands. However, it unfortunately means that people are doing their paperwork again, so back to the typewriter.

We seem to have found ourselves quite a good niche here, organising all the merchantmen . . . organising a programme of refuelling, passing on their signals using our satellite equipment, allocating areas to keep to, and generally shepherding them around . . . . The Captain received a note from the Admiral's Staff Officer Operations, saying, "Thank you for all the good work you are doing in the TRALA. I hope it is not too dull". We can put up with some dullness quite easily, thank you!

As we were the only destroyer left down here (out of the five which originally came down) we were quite glad to take a breather for a while, and as we had fired 1,300 rounds it will take the reinforcements a while to catch up with our total – although as *Cardiff* fired 270 last night she can't be far behind.

It is very busy on the Flight Deck as the helicopter is always in use, ferrying stores around, and often we take stores to give to another ship somewhere else . . . . It is very interesting seeing all the different types of ship. *Canberra* was alongside today, with quite a few rust-streaks on her beautiful white paintwork. And there are North Sea ferries, tankers, landing ships, and our usual oilers and store ships around. Plenty of them too. It is still quite pleasant on the upper deck. Today was a crisp, bright December day, and on the Flight Deck there is always some shelter from the wind.

Even out here, two hundred miles away from land, there is still a surprisingly large number of sea birds, and not especially large ones, too. I suppose when they get tired they simply sit on the water. Last week we had a couple of quite tame white seagulls who used to like walking up and down the Flight Deck, looking for interesting morsels. We left some bread out for them, and one even ate from the aircrewman's hand. However, after a few days of bread they wanted something better (just like cats!). Maybe they were hoping for a tasty bit of fish from the galley.

We don't have much news from ashore. It's not like [here in] the Navy when every latest snippet is flashed around the Fleet on the radio nets instantly. We have often heard news from a destroyer two hundred miles away while their missiles are still in flight. Most of the news of troop movements we hear from the BBC, although the detailed dispositions do filter back to us eventually. What does annoy me is when Mr Nott, or the press reporters, announce something that is just about to happen *as it is happening*, at that moment: taking all the kudos for some poor bloke in a slit trench who has then got to fight like mad to make it all come true. I know that the people at home seem wholeheartedly in support of the Forces here, as is borne out by the generosity in giving to the South Atlantic Fund. But it does seem totally despicable that the politicians should have any glory when it is their mess we have to sort out. If they had sent Hercules aircraft to Stanley with the spearhead battalion on March 31st there would not now be 6,000 British troops trying to retake the wretched place. The Conservatives' recent by-election victories really make me annoyed. I was glad to see that both David Steel and the Baptists said the whole thing should be sorted out peacefully.

You seem to be very busy . . . with the proofs of your book, tending to the veggies, and visiting lots of interesting old farmhouses. The descriptions you sent conjured up a lovely picture of Beatrix Potter-type Lakeland scenes (I saw a Beatrix Potter exhibition in Edinburgh – where we called after yet another exercise – in February, where they had the original watercolours of Peter Rabbit . . . strange, to think that these were the actual drawings from which the prints were taken) . . . .

That's about all the news from here at the moment. Life is very nicely routine here, and everybody is very relaxed and very well. We recently had first crack at a store ship straight out from England, so we are all topped up with food and goodies. We have ice cream for lunch and have even had some apples. The last store ship really used up everything. They even found some butter which had turned green although deep-frozen. It had been laid down as "emergency war stocks" when the ship first commissioned. Incidentally, that was the store ship which sailed to the Gulf with us and was just about to go home from Gibraltar when we were all sent here. She has been away since October 19th, so they will be very glad to get home.

Lots of love for now; I will write again soon.

**HMS GLAMORGAN**

*Killed in Action, 12 June 1982*

Michael Adcock, Petty Officer, aged 34
Brian Easton, Cook, aged 24
Mark Henderson, Air Engineering Mechanic, aged 20
Brian Hinge, Air Engineering Mechanic, aged 24
David Lee, Acting Chief Engineering Mechanic, aged 35
Kelvin McCullum, Air Engineering Artificer, aged 25
Brian Malcolm, Cook, aged 22
Terry Perkins, Marine Engineering Mechanic, aged 19
Mark Sambles, Leading Cook, aged 29
Tony Sillence, Leading Cook, aged 26
John Stroud, Steward, aged 20
David Tinker, Lieutenant, aged 25
Colin Vickers, Petty Officer, aged 33

Committed to the ocean deep in position 51° 50′ 50″ South, 53° 31′ 80″ West. 160 miles East of Falkland Islands: on the evening of 12 June.

It was hoped to conclude with some of the poems David wrote in the intervals of the Falklands fighting. The evidence that he was again writing poetry comes from two of his friends in *Glamorgan* who often saw David composing his poems on the Flight Deck. They were just on slips of paper as he had insufficient time to copy them into a book. We were eagerly looking forward to reading them when his possessions were returned. Not until three months after David's death did the Navy deliver his papers and his kit to Christine. There were no poems.

Inquiries from his friends produced the suggestion that he had kept the poems in the carrier of his respirator. The ship's company were required to have their respirators by them at all times. Most put additional oddments into the carrier – a bar of chocolate, a treasured photograph, a letter or two – in case they had suddenly to abandon ship. At the time of the Exocet attack, David's respirator was hanging in the small office off the hangar, which was badly burnt, almost certainly consuming the respirator bag. If this is what actually happened, then the Exocet not only destroyed Dave's life but also any possibility of literary immortality. Of his spiritual immortality we do not doubt.

Let us end instead with lines which David himself chose for his epitaph. When the ships were waiting near Ascension Island, everyone was required to make out a Will to be returned to Britain. With his Will, David included certain instructions in case of his death. He asked, if he were to be buried in earth, for an inscription to be placed on his grave. These are among the last words written by Rupert Brooke – 'Fragments written during the voyage to Gallipoli April 1915' and David must have considered that his voyage might have the same ending.

Here is the passage which Christine showed to David's parents in the cottage at Clungunford:

> *He wears*
> *The ungathered blossom of quiet; stiller he*
> *Than a deep well at noon, or lovers met,*
> *Than sleep, or the heart after wrath. He is*
> *The silence following great words of peace.*

Let this be his parting word